INSURANCE BILLING BASICS

Steps for Therapists to Successfully Take Insurance

Co-Authored by Jeremy Zug, Kathryn Zug, and Kate Perry

WHO IS THIS BOOK FOR?

Working with mental health clinicians, we've encountered so many providers who have a passion for their patients, are dedicated to their field, and want to make a difference in the lives of others. The insurance billing process often stands in the way of these providers achieving these goals, creating headaches, sleepless nights, and anxiety over running a practice. Every provider is capable of running a financially viable practice that accomplishes the therapeutic mission with the right knowledge and tools.

This resource is for mental health clinicians who have recently completed grad school and want an introduction to insurance billing, who are starting their private practice, who are new to accepting insurance for their patients, or who are experiencing chronic issues with their insurance billing.

In the healthcare industry, very few educational resources are about the revenue cycle and revenue cycle management for private practices. Our goal is to educate providers so that they can make the best decisions for their practice. Our expertise comes from our billing services that remove much of the burden of insurance billing from providers like you. This resource was developed by collating and expanding upon topics that we had written about on our blog, placing them into a framework that gives a big picture on insurance billing in private practice. Even if they are using our billing services, we always encourage providers to be educated on what their biller is doing and how it helps their business. We would be honored if you choose us as your billing partner.

Most importantly, we want you to understand the insurance billing process and make decisions with all available information. You care for the future of your practice, and so do we!

Our mission is to empower you to focus on patient care by educating you about best practices in the revenue cycle management process. We want to create and communicate clarity in a confusing, frustrating, outdated industry. Health insurance and reimbursement do not have to be the elusive creature you may fear or think it is. Practice Solutions can help you on your insurance journey in whatever capacity we can, beginning with this book. It is one of the most thorough treatments on insurance billing for beginners, compiled using our experience helping thousands of providers with their insurance billing. We wish we had this book when we were starting!

This book was designed by Practice Solutions to give you both a high-level overview of the insurance billing process and more detailed instructions on how to manage each stage within your private practice. We used a textbook-style format to deliver the information in a way that we felt made sense, with concepts and principles building on each other as you read the book. We started with basics and then dug deeper as we went.

For this book, we assume that you already are established with an NPI, tax ID, and articles of incorporation for your business. If not, you can use these instructions on how to apply for an NPI (https://nppes.cms.hhs.gov/assets/How_to_apply_for_an_NPI_online.pdf) or this NPI application form (https://www.cms.gov/medicare/cms-forms/cms-forms/downloads/cms10114.pdf) that can be mailed. You can reference these instructions to apply for an EIN number (https://www.irs.gov/businesses/small-businesses-self-employed/get-an-employer-identification-number). You should learn to register your business within your state and follow those procedures. We intend that you use the information in this book to inform the development of your processes for insurance billing within your private practice and to use this information to help you make the best choices for your business. The ultimate goal is that this book enables you to develop a successful therapy business, serving the population you want to serve while bringing in reliable payment from insurance.

Each chapter of the book will end with action items that you can do based on the knowledge that you learned. These action items are meant to help you set up a process for revenue cycle management that works for you and your practice. We recommend reading this book in companion with a blank notebook where you can plan.

At the end of this book, we hope that you have a clear understanding of insurance billing from start to finish, who the key players are in the process and that you feel confident in revenue cycle management so that you can work with your patients at the practice of your dreams.

INDEX

Chapter 1:

THE BASIC PROCESS OF WORKING WITH INSURANCE 7

Chapter 2:

DECIDING WHICH INSURANCE PAYERS TO WORK WITH 24

    The Most Profitable Mixes......................... 26

    The Fewer the Insurance Companies the Better (But Meet Your Goals!) 33

Chapter 3:

HOW TO GET CREDENTIALED.................... 46

    Credential Yourself 47

    Outsourcing 47

Chapter 4:

PREPARATION FOR BILLING...................... 70

Chapter 5:

ESTABLISHING PATIENT RELATIONSHIPS 84

Chapter 6:
ELIGIBILITY AND BENEFIT CHECKS 99

Chapter 7:
COMPLETING SESSIONS 118

Chapter 8:
RCM STAGE 4: CLAIM SUBMISSION 132

Chapter 9:
RCM STAGE 5: PAYMENT POSTING 150

Chapter 10:
RCM STAGE 6: CLAIM FOLLOW-UP 166

Chapter 11:
RCM STAGE 7: OUTSTANDING PATIENT COLLECTIONS 178

Chapter 12:
FINAL THOUGHTS 185

GLOSSARY 187

Chapter 1:
THE BASIC PROCESS OF WORKING WITH INSURANCE

First, let's take a look at a general overview of the billing process. We've broken this down into two categories: **Credentialing**, which would take place before any claim submission but is integral to the billing process, and **Billing**, otherwise known as **Revenue Cycle Management**.

Understanding these two principles and how they relate will be key to your success as a private practice accepting insurance and will put you ahead of the rest.

CREDENTIALING

Defining Credentialing

Credentialing is the process by which a provider becomes **In-Network** with an insurance plan and, through that affiliation, can accept third-party payment. For an insurance company to allow you into their network and establish a contract with you for service reimbursement, they must verify your credentials such as proof of education, NPI, Tax Information, business name and address, among other information - hence the name credentialing. Credentialing should be completed before accepting insurance patients and before any insurance billing occurs for the smoothest billing experience.

Paneling is another name for the credentialing process, since as a result of credentialing you are added to the insurance company's panel. An **insurance panel**, also known as a **provider panel**, is a list of healthcare providers (including therapists) who are approved to provide in-network services to patients under a specific insurance plan.

An Overview of the Credentialing Process

To become credentialed with an insurance company, you will first want to confirm with provider services that each network you want to join is accepting new providers. If they are, you will need to complete an application with each insurance company you would like to become credentialed with. The easiest way to obtain these applications is to go to an insurance company's website and locate their provider resources area. From there, you may be able to download an application or get in touch with someone in the provider services area of the insurance company who can assist you in obtaining an application.

Once you have an application, you can complete the application with all of the requested information. The application includes your **NPI number**, **tax ID**, business name, and business address. It is important to note that whatever information you submit on your credentialing application will be expected to match what you submit on future insurance claims. You will want to have a record of the information you submitted and make any updates, such as a change in address, with the insurance company when necessary. In the application process, the insurance company may request copies of various forms of identification, which we will cover in-depth in Chapter 3.

Upon completion of the application (and triple-checking everything), it is sent to the insurance company, and it can generally take between six months and one year for your application to be reviewed and processed. This timeline is variable depending on many factors, such as the insurance company's application volume, processing time, and the accuracy of your documentation submission. If accepted, you will receive notice and a contract to review, sign, and return to the insurance company. The insurance company will then process the contract and notify you when you are officially In-Network. You should be provided with a copy of the finalized contract, signed by both you and the insurance company that you need to save to your records for future reference. It is at this point that you would be able to begin billing for insurance.

How Often Do You Complete Credentialing?

If you want to accept insurance from your patients, credentialing should happen before billing. Once credentialed, you must comply with any re-verification requirements outlined by the insurance company to ensure that all of your information is still valid. You must complete the re-verification process even if none of your information has changed. This process allows the insurance company to confirm that you are still an active provider and want to remain on their list of in-network providers. Most insurance companies require re-verifying your credentialing at varying frequencies, but you will typically need to renew your credentialing after three years.

The re-verification process is simple if all of your information is the same. Just make sure that you complete it! Look out for any notices from the insurance company, or note the timeframe for re-verification designated in your contract and be proactive about completing it with the insurance company. If you do not re-verify, you will likely be removed as an in network provider with the insurance company and a new application would need to be submitted.

Suppose any of the following information has changed. In that case, you will need to update your existing credentialing:

- Your Practice Address
- Your Practice Name
- Your Name (common reasons include marriage and divorce)
- Your Tax ID (This would typically be to correct an error, or if you decide to change from using your SSN to an EIN and all other information remains the same)
- Your NPI (This would typically be to correct an error)

If any of these circumstances apply to you, you will need to submit an entirely new credentialing application:

- You previously worked for a group practice credentialed under their group NPI and Tax ID and you now work under your practice
- You previously worked for a group practice credentialed under their group NPI and Tax ID and you now work for a different group practice. Consult your new employer on their credentialing processes
- Your practice has moved from one state to another
- You were credentialed as an individual and would like to credential your practice as a group using a type 2 NPI

Can You Bill Insurance Without Credentialing?

If you decide to send claims to an insurance company without credentialing, this is called **Out-of-Network** billing. Out-of-network simply means you are not contracted with an insurance company. As a result, claims you send to an insurance company you are not contracted with will be processed according to a different level of benefits for your patient. In most cases, out-of-network claims are processed with a much higher deductible or will be denied outright, leaving your patient to pay the bill for services as if they are a private pay patient.

When billing out-of-network, you still need to prove that you are a qualified and licensed mental health provider with documentation, often requiring submission of a W-2 form, so the insurance companies can issue a reimbursement. You are not held to their specific contract or contracted insurance rates that you are with your in-network contract.

BILLING: REVENUE CYCLE MANAGEMENT

Defining Billing

After you have credentialed and received your contract with the insurance company, you are ready to begin billing! **Billing** is submitting the necessary information to a patient's insurance company regarding their session so that a provider can receive reimbursement for services rendered. Throughout this book, we hope to clarify what billing means and the steps you need to take to complete insurance billing successfully.

Stages of Revenue Cycle Management

The billing process can be broken down into seven stages, starting with the first interaction with a patient before any therapy session takes place, all the way through to collecting payment for services rendered. As you begin billing, you will start to have many claims at various stages in the billing process, and you will want to track each claim's stage and take specific actions based on the stage the claim is in. In the billing world, we call this **Revenue Cycle Management**.

Revenue Cycle Management is managed through software systems known as **Electronic Health Record** systems or **EHRs**. Electronic Health Record systems are tools designed for healthcare providers to store patient data, schedule appointments, complete progress notes, and generate and submit claims. You may also see them referred to as Electronic Medical Records, or EMR, which is another term for the same type of software. Throughout this book, we will be using the term EHR.

For now, we will define each stage in the revenue cycle management process. In later chapters, we will cover more in-depth practices that you can implement to ensure that each stage runs smoothly.

Stage 1: Pre-registration

Pre-registration is the term used to describe the process that is followed when a potential new patient or representative of the patient calls into your office. It is an information-gathering phase, where you and the potential patient learn about each other, deciding whether or not the relationship is a good fit. Pre-registration spans from when the potential patient first contacts you up to the point that they come in for their appointment.

If the potential new patient is ready to schedule an appointment after learning about your practice, you will need to collect information about the **patient**, the person you will be treating, and the **subscriber**, or the insurance policy holder. The patient and subscriber are often the same person, but could be different if the patient is a dependent of the subscriber. You would collect the following information:

- Patient Full Legal Name (Verify Spelling)
- Patient Date of Birth
- Subscriber Full Name
- Subscriber Date of Birth
- Subscriber Social Security Number
- Subscriber relationship to patient
- Patient Address
- Patient's Insurance Carrier and Plan. If possible, have the patient submit a photo of the front and back of their insurance card to you
- Photo of the Patient's Driver's License or ID (if possible)
- Treatment that the patient is seeking
- Signed HIPAA Consent Form
- Signed Financial Policy
- Signed Payment Information Form

The pre-registration phase is the first interaction between you and your patient. It is a great time to establish your brand with potential patients and set expectations for their treatment process. Your process should be personal and specific to your practice.

In this stage, you will also want to complete an **eligibility and benefits check** (E&B Check) for your patient by contacting their insurance provider to verify their benefits and coverage for your services. An eligibility check will tell you whether or not the patient's insurance will cover this service, and a benefit check will tell you what a patient would owe for their visit and inform you what to expect regarding billing. Eligibility and benefit checks are an estimate provided by the insurance company, and may process differently at the time of claim submission. This is not to diminish their importance (they are extremely important), but to warn you that the information provided by the insurance company is not always correct. E&B Checks can also be referred to as a **Verification of Benefits**, or VOB.

If any portion of the patient's demographic information is incorrect an eligibility and benefits check cannot be performed until the correct information has been obtained. This is why we recommend collecting a picture of the front and back of the patient's insurance card along with their driver's license; accuracy and attention to detail are crucial at this stage. If you cannot do an eligibility and benefits check at this point, you can do so during the registration phase but it is always preferable to have the eligibility and benefit check completed before the patient arrives in your office.

Stage 2: Registration

Registration is the term used to describe the process when the patient is physically present in your office and allows you to verify some of the information collected in pre-registration with physical documents.

Registration is the most important step in the process. You are making a first impression on your new patients and the community and gathering the necessary information to submit a **clean claim**, or a claim that processes on its initial submission.

- In the registration process, you should verify the following with your patient in-office:
- You have a signed **HIPAA consent form** on file for the patient
- You have reviewed and collected a copy of your office's **financial policy** signed by the patient
- You have a copy of the patient's payment information to be kept on file to charge the patient when necessary
- You have a copy of the front and back of the patient's current **insurance card** and driver's license
- All information that you collected in the pre-registration phase is correct, and you have collected any necessary information that was missed during pre-registration
- All information has been entered into your **EHR** system and is entered correctly

If you have not yet done an eligibility and benefits check, you would need to do so now. It is always better to complete an E&B check in the pre-registration phase, before the patient is in your office, so that you can be fully prepared to collect any necessary payment.

Stage 3: Charge Capture

Charge Capture is the stage where you get paid by your patient. Using the information you learned from the eligibility and benefit check performed in the registration phase, you can charge the patient for what they owe for the session according to their benefit plan. The amount you collect may be the full contracted amount for the session according to your insurance fee schedule which gets applied to the patient's deductible, a copay or coinsurance amount, or nothing, depending on the patient's insurance plan. You must do your best to collect the correct payment from the patient at the time of service to maintain your contractual obligation with the insurance company and ensure that you receive proper reimbursement for your services.

Stage 4: Claim Submission

Between Charge Capture and Claim Submission, a few steps need to occur that aren't necessarily part of the billing process. Firstly, you need to complete the therapy session with your patient and record it in your EHR with the proper coding. Second, you need to complete your notes for the session. Both of these are covered in more detail in Chapter 7. Only after completing your notes can you move on to Claim Submission.

Claim submission is the process by which all information about your session with a patient is transmitted to the insurance company so that the insurance company can review and remit any necessary payment. After the session has occurred and entered into the EHR, the necessary bits of information are compiled into a claim. The claim can be a hard copy form CMS-1500 or an electronic version called an **Electronic Data Interchange (EDI)**. Your paper claims can be mailed and EDI claims can be submitted electronically depending on the insurance companies requirements.

Stage 5: Payment Posting

This step describes recording payment from the insurance company. Payment Posting is tedious work and should be completed by someone with the time, technical knowledge, and attention to detail to ensure this process is well-executed. Every insurance transaction should come with a document known as an **explanation of benefits (EOB)** or **electronic remittance advice (ERA)**. The terms EOB and ERA represent the same thing: a piece of documentation outlining patients and dates of service that have been processed for payment together, or that have not been processed for payment due to a denial. For each patient and date of service represented on the EOB or ERA, further information can be found about how their benefits were processed and paid according to their benefits, or reasons for denials.

Each insurance company has its own "language" for these documents, using similar but different terms to describe errors and denials. Each EOB is formatted differently as well.

When posting payments, claims will either be resolved and closed if the full payment has been made, left open with outstanding patient balances, or the EOB or ERA may provide information about a denial. Claims that are closed do not move on to stages 6 and 7, their revenue cycle is complete. For any rejected or denied claims, you will want to have someone dedicated to resolving these issues in stage 6, Claim Follow-Up. If a claim has an outstanding patient balance, it may skip stage 6 and move directly to stage 7, Patient Collections.

Stage 6: Claim Follow-Up

Claim Follow-Up is the process that takes outstanding claims and finds resolution to those claims in collaboration with the insurance company. Each insurance company has a different appeal or claim correction process that you must know and understand.

Claim Follow-Up is also when most of a clinician's time is wasted on administrative work. It is common for someone to spend hours on the phone with the insurance company only to find unclarity.

If the insurance company doesn't pay your claims, then there is an issue somewhere in the process. Following up on claims allows you to resolve issues with current claims, and identify issues in the process to prevent errors on future claims.

Stage 7: Patient Collections

Patient collections is the process where the practice collects outstanding amounts that went uncollected from patients. Outstanding balances can happen if an eligibility and benefits check is not performed before a session and you don't know what to charge the patient during Charge Capture, or if a patient has moved from one level of their benefits to the next (i.e. a deductible or out of pocket maximum was met during the processing of this claim). If the information received from the eligibility and benefits check is incorrect, the claim will process differently than what was collected and your patient could owe a balance or need to be issued a credit. If money is not collected from the patient during the Charge Capture phase for any other reason, your patient owes a balance.

Patient collections can be as simple as calling a patient to authorize processing a payment on a credit card that is kept on file, or can involve sending mail, email and text reminders with methods for the patient to submit payment. In the worst case scenario, the provider retains the services of a collections agency who will take further action to collect money from a patient who is no longer receiving counseling services and has unpaid balances. Ideally, you won't have to get to this stage in the process, but if you do there are good resources available to help with patient collections

THE ETHICS OF INSURANCE BILLING

Billing is not just about getting paid. Being an In-Network Provider and accepting patients with insurance plans demands a level of ethical responsibility. You have entered a contractual agreement with the insurance company to submit claims in a timely manner, and follow all of the necessary requirements to record sessions with patients properly. You also have a responsibility to your patients to submit these claims so that their insurance plans are properly updated, and that all costs related to your service are accurately collected according to their insurance plan.

PRACTICE SOLUTIONS: YOUR REVENUE CYCLE MANAGEMENT PARTNER

This book is meant to provide you with an understanding of how billing works, and the knowledge to complete your own billing. However, thousands of therapists have benefitted from the time that they get back when they outsource their billing to the professionals at Practice Solutions. We have assembled a team of expert billers located within the United States to assist with almost all stages of the Revenue Cycle Management Process. We have celebrated with providers who have gotten their first restful sleep in months, providers who received outstanding claims revenue to cover the cost of their vacation and more (all while they were on vacation), and who have grown their practice to the point where they were ready to manage their billing in-house.

There are three ways that you can utilize Practice Solutions as a Revenue Cycle Management Partner. The first is by engaging with our educational materials; reading this book, and subscribing to our blog. You can learn more about effective billing through these resources and use what you learn in practical application.

The second is to sign up for billing services where we manage Eligibility and Benefit checks with honed experience of knowing what to ask to get the most accurate benefit information for you. We help you keep your patient's insurance information accurate in your EHR system. We ensure that all claims that are ready to submit are submitted in a timely manner and reviewed with the trained eye of a biller. We manage payment posting, interpreting ERAs to understand denials, and perform follow-up on all claims including claim rejections. We offer options that allow us to process patient payments and facilitate patient collections as well.

The third option is through our Practice Health Checks and Professional Services. Practice Health Checks are an annual analysis of seven domains related to insurance billing. Your practice's performance is graded in relation to your goals and industry standards to present a clear picture of how your insurance billing processes are performing. If any areas are not performing optimally, you can then opt to purchase relevant training sessions, documents, process creations or consultations that are designed to improve your billing processes.

We hope that with the information in this book, you are either empowered to manage your own insurance billing, or you are empowered to partner with Practice Solutions and make the most out of a provider-biller relationship with your understanding of the billing process.

CHAPTER SUMMARY

If you would like to run a private practice that accepts insurance, there are two phases of work that need to be completed: Credentialing (one time application with recurring verification) and Billing (an ongoing process with 7 stages that must be evaluated for each session you complete). At this point in the process you are learning about the high-level process of billing and credentialing.

Follow-Up Actions to Take

- Train your staff on the high-level stages of billing and credentialing. You will retain most of what you teach
- Journal about the customer experience with your practice and how you would like the insurance process to look and feel
- Document the flow of information in your practice to gain clarity around how billing works in your office
- Compile a list of the gaps in your knowledge and how you might find the answer to those gaps

Now that you have an understanding of the relationship between credentialing and billing and a general idea of those processes, we would like to provide some food for thought on getting your practice ready for insurance billing. By working with thousands of providers over the years, we've gained insight into what works for insurance based practices, and what doesn't. In the next chapter, we will ask you to do some reflecting on goals for your practice, and provide strategies on how to decide which insurance payers to work with.

Chapter 2:
DECIDING WHICH INSURANCE PAYERS TO WORK WITH

Most clinicians begin formulating which insurance companies they want to accept early in their counseling career based on preconceived notions that may or may not be the best choice for their practice. We would like to offer an academic and forensic approach to choosing which insurance companies you would like to work with. We want to encourage you to set aside your own predilections about specific insurance companies. Instead, focus on where you want to be in the future and how you can use insurance as a vehicle to accomplish those goals.

There are two stages to deciding which insurances you would like to work with. The first is to determine your insurance mix, or how many payers you work with, which types of payers you want to work with, and how many insurance patients you want to accept versus private pay patients. Determining your insurance mix is more about a broader business strategy for your practice and establishing goals. The second stage is identifying the exact insurance companies that can help you achieve the goals that you set.

THE VALUE OF GOAL SETTING

Before you start credentialing with every insurance company possible, we encourage you to sit down and really evaluate your goals for your practice. These goals can include things like how many hours a week you would like to work, revenue goals, goals for growth, and goals for your physical practice location. All of these goals can help inform your strategy for accepting (or not accepting) insurance.

No goal is too small or too big- if you want it, write it down! Understanding what your ideal practice looks will help you as you make decisions for your practice. With each choice you face, you can ask yourself "does this move me closer to my goals?"

DETERMINING YOUR INSURANCE MIX

When we talk about your insurance mix, we are talking about the strategic decision of how many insurances you accept, and how much of your patient base is insurance versus private pay. There are three strategies of accepting insurance that we most commonly see our clients use that are the most successful. By successful, we mean most profitable. Which strategy you employ will be driven by your goals for your practice.

The Most Profitable Mixes

Plan 1: The Lean Plan

The Lean Plan is simple; take the smallest amount of in-network payers as possible with higher levels of reimbursement. In this scenario you have evaluated the highest paying insurance companies in your area and you are only going to engage with those 1 or 2 insurance companies. This could mean that you are only in-network with one commercial payer and one government payer or just one to two commercial payers.

The main advantage of the Lean Plan is that it allows you to maximize your average reimbursement rate per hour, which can have a big impact on your practice's annual revenue. Each insurance company sets its own reimbursement rates, and those can vary widely. As an example, let's look at the hypothetical table of reimbursement rates for a 60 minute session, identified by the billing code 90837, below.

Insurance Company A	$145.20
Insurance Company B	$132.10
Insurance Company C	$66.40
Insurance Company D	$101.20
Insurance Company E	$87.65
Insurance Company F	$77.42
Insurance Company G	$190.90
Insurance Company H	$45.50
Insurance Company I	$98.78

| Insurance Company J | $120.20 |
| Insurance Company K | $76.50 |

One therapist decides to utilize the Lean Plan, and only credentials with Insurance company A, B and C. Assuming an equal number of patients from each insurance company, they can assume an average hourly reimbursement rate of $114.57. This was calculated by adding the reimbursement rates for insurance companies A, B and C and dividing by 3.

A second therapist in the same area decided to credential with every insurance company on the list. To calculate their average hourly reimbursement, we added every reimbursement rate in the list and divided that sum by 11 insurance companies. Again assuming an equal number of patients from each insurance company, they can assume an average hourly reimbursement rate of $103.80.

This means that the first therapist has the potential to make on average $10.77 more per hour than the second therapist. That difference is more than the federal minimum wage.

At face value, this does not sound like a lot of money. However, let's do some additional math that will help highlight the vast disparity that $10.77 makes in the life of a practice.

Let's say each therapist sees 20 patients per week and takes 4 weeks of vacation a year. The therapists each work 48 weeks of the year seeing patients.

20 patients per week X 48 weeks of the year = 960 sessions per year

First Therapist: 960 sessions X $114.57 = $109,987.20 per year in pre-tax income

Second Therapist: 960 sessions X 103.80 = $99,648.00 per year in pre-tax income

The first therapist makes $10,339.20 more per year than the second therapist. That is the difference for just a solo provider. The numbers become even more significant when you are looking at a group practice.

The downside with the Lean Plan is that you may have to make decisions based on guesswork of reimbursement rates since rates for private insurance companies are not public information. You also are accepting the risk that if the payer experiences any problems, such as a cyber attack that impacts their ability to accept and reimburse claims, you may have a disruption of cash flow. The Lean Plan may also limit the number of highly-clinical patients that you take and that can be counterintuitive to your reason for getting involved in private practice in the first place. If you want to help more of the highly clinical patients, you may be more interested in the second strategy to take insurance and remain profitable, which we call The Focused Plan.

Plan 2: The Focused Plan

The Focused Plan involves maintaining a health profit margin while focusing on particular clinical objectives in your private practice. Let's say you have a heart for geriatric populations; it is important that you take Medicare in your private practice. Or perhaps you LOVE working with veterans and active-duty military personnel and you absolutely must be in-network with Tricare.

This is totally doable and highly encouraged! We love the passion and we love the big "whys" to be involved in the private practice industry.

The Focused Plan allows you to accomplish those clinical objectives and still work with those patients that fit squarely into your purpose for private practice by developing a balanced case load of higher paying commercial insurance patients, private pay patients, and lower paying government insurance

This approach helps you to take insurance and be profitable, but involves tracking the risk around your caseload. In this strategy, you need to do some math and manage your caseload so you can maintain your profitability and achieve your personal practice goals. This depends on your state because reimbursement rates vary across states and payers, but this is a good starting point for the breakdown for your caseload:

    40% Commercial Insurance with an average reimbursement between $85.00 and $125.00 per session

10% Private Pay with an average reimbursement between $100.00 and $150.00 per session

50% Government Insurance with an average reimbursement between $55.00 and $85.00 per session.

Let's break that down in terms of real numbers assuming that an average weekly caseload for a full-time clinician is 25 patients or 5 patients per day.

12 commercial insurance patients per week that net $1260.00 (i.e. $105.00 per session)

2 private pay patients per week that net $250.00 (i.e. $125.00 per session)

13 government insurance patients per week that net $780.00 (i.e. $60.00 per session)

Using this per week model, your full-time caseload should bring in $2,290.00 per week or $9,847.00 per month and still favor those populations that you want to work with clinically. You can play with the percentages of patient types internally to achieve your goals, but this example demonstrates that it is mathematically possible to spend half of your clinical time focused on those populations that you are passionate about and still maintain healthy profitability.

In order for this plan to be successful, you will need to be disciplined about the patients that you take on, monitor your percentages, and be sure you are actually collecting from your private pay patients, commercial and government insurance patients.

One challenge to overcome with this model is that as you scale you would also have to monitor your clinicians to make sure you are balancing their caseloads as well.

Plan 3: The Hamburger Plan

The last strategy is something that we have dubbed the Hamburger Plan because it involves a mix of both In-Network and Out-of-Network plans, referencing a popular fast food burger chain In-n-Out. The Hamburger Plan is similar to the Lean Plan in that you take 1 or 2 insurances that yield the greatest reimbursement, but this strategy also includes having out-of-network billing status with a multitude of insurance companies. While we have seen providers employ this strategy successfully, it is our least preferred strategy out of the three that we have presented as the benefits are not as great as with the first two strategies.

There are two primary benefits of billing out-of-network with patients. You can continue to accept patients with an out-of-network insurance company, and the claims won't be denied outright. Instead, when you submit a claim to the insurance company, the insurance company is going to process the claim as an out of network claim and apply the claim to the out of network benefits for your patient. In this scenario, the claim is going to likely apply to the patient's out-of-network deductible. Over time, the patient may satisfy the out of network deductible leading to a lower cost-share for the patient, though this is unlikely. Being an out-of-network provider is useful if you have patients you are treating who have recently changed insurance plans, or if you specialize in treatments that are not as widely available in your area.

The second benefit of becoming an out of network provider with any number of insurance providers is that you are not held to the same contractual agreements as an in-network provider. You are not held to contracted rates as you are when you are an in-network provider, allowing you to offer a **sliding scale of rates** to out-of-network patients. A sliding scale allows you to set different rates for patients based on their income level, offering affordable options for care. By providing benefits to patients on an out-of-network basis, you open your patients up to the potential for using their insurance while releasing your practice from the same requirements as an in-network provider.

If you are using this strategy, there is still an administrative burden to get clinicians listed as out-of-network but it is far less than the credentialing process for in-network credentialing. Another important concern is that your practice has to be uniquely skilled at collecting from patients at the time of service, each and every session.

The Fewer the Insurance Companies the Better (But Meet Your Goals!)

As a mental health therapist, starting your own practice can be a challenging but rewarding experience. You may have noticed a common theme among each of the suggested plans above: they all involve selecting a few insurance companies to be in-network with. While it may seem like credentialing with as many insurance companies as possible will lead to more patients and a more profitable practice, there are actually several benefits to keeping your in-network options limited.

Reduced Administrative Burden

When you limit the number of insurance companies you work with, you'll have less administrative work to do. Each insurance company will have its own requirements for credentialing, billing, and documentation. By keeping the number of insurance companies small, you can streamline your administrative tasks and focus on providing quality care to your patients. This means you'll spend less time on paperwork and more time doing what you love – helping people.

Your overall billing processes will be leaner and simpler. Billing and insurance-related costs for a private practice owner revolve around claims submission, claims reconciliation, and payment processing.

By engaging one to two insurance companies on an in-network basis you only need to learn one to two processes for each stage of Revenue Cycle Management. This delays and reduces your administrative burden and allows you to operate as simply as possible.

Here are some examples of what we mean:

- You only need to learn how to read 1 or 2 types of insurance cards and input information into your EHR accordingly
- You only need to understand two sets of fee schedules
- You only need to learn to read two different types of EOB/ERAs with their corresponding portals
- You only need to understand the process of Eligibility and Benefits checks for two different insurance companies

This list is not exhaustive, but provides you with a general idea of the administrative burden we are talking about.

More Control Over Your Practice

When you're not credentialing with a high number of insurance companies, you have more control over your practice. For example, you can set your own private pay rates and decide how many of each private pay and insurance patients you want to see in a week. You won't be limited as much by the reimbursement rates set by insurance companies, and you can choose to work with patients who are a good fit for your practice, rather than just those who are covered by a particular insurance plan. This can lead to a more fulfilling and satisfying practice.

Easily Scale Your Business

Let's say you are starting to scale in terms of adding clinical staff. It is much MUCH easier to credential 10 clinicians with 1 insurance than 10 clinicians with 10 insurances. This benefit can be better understood by looking at the math in terms of individual panels that you credential therapists with.

10 providers credentialed with one insurance company means 10 credentialing applications to complete. 10 providers each being credentialed with 10 insurance companies means 100 separate credentialing applications to complete.

Your expenses will increase if you have to engage in 100 credentialing activities versus 10 credentialing activities. Many credentialers will charge a set fee per panel, or if you are credentialing yourself the cost is the hours that will be put into filling out applications and following up on your application status. If you are a group practice this becomes even more important because the complexity of credentialing and paneling only increases as you grow.

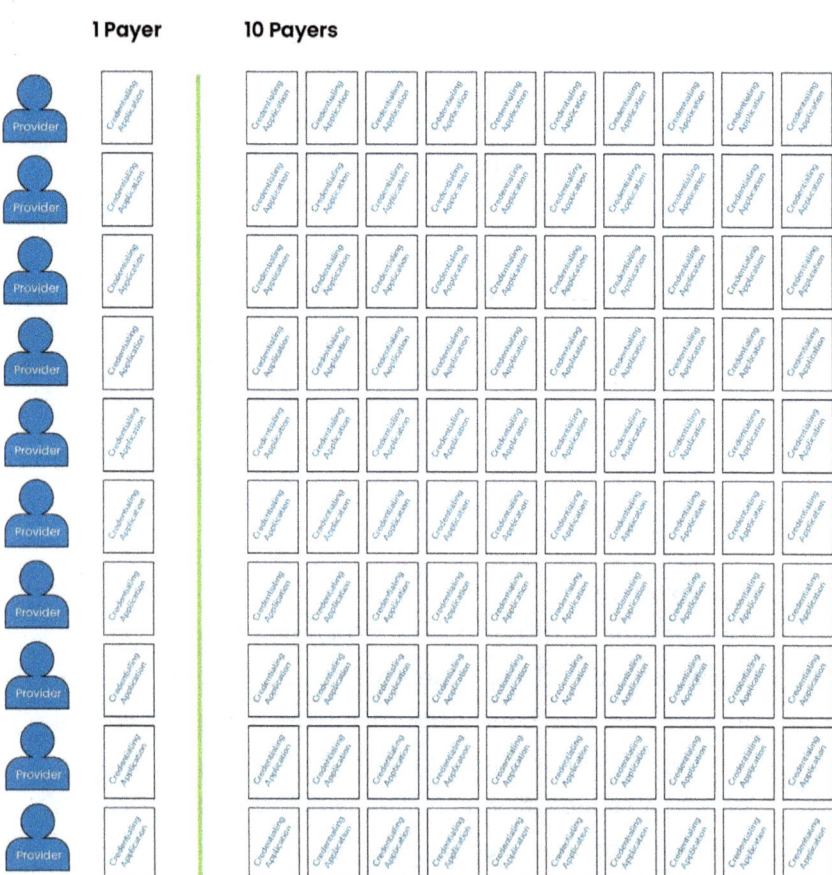

Better Relationships with Patients

Finally, by not credentialing with a high number of insurance companies, you can build better relationships with your patients. When you have a comprehensive understanding of the insurance company's processes and policies you can clearly and effectively communicate with your patients about their insurance coverage, any payments owed, and guide them if they need to contact the insurance company directly. This is much easier to manage with one to two insurance companies than it is with a dozen. When patients are held accountable for their portion of healthcare costs, they can be more invested in the therapeutic process. They are more likely to attend sessions regularly, participate fully in therapy, and make progress towards their goals. Additionally, when you're not overwhelmed by navigating insurance company policies and procedures, you can provide more personalized and flexible care to your patients. This can lead to better outcomes and a stronger therapeutic alliance.

While it may be tempting to credential with as many insurance companies as possible when starting your practice, limiting the number of in-network options can actually be beneficial. By reducing administrative work, increasing control over your practice, and building better relationships with your patients, you can create a more fulfilling and successful practice. So when making the decision to credential with insurance companies, consider the benefits of keeping the number small.

IDENTIFYING YOUR BEST INSURANCE PARTNERS

One question that we see quite frequently from private practice owners is "Which insurance company is the best to work with?" This is something that we are unable to answer directly, because the answer is unique to each practice. What we can do is provide some suggestions of factors to consider when you are deciding which insurance companies to work with. Consider each of the concepts below when researching insurance companies to help you find the best insurance partners for your practice.

Research Potential Insurance Partners

Before you look internally at your practice's goals and objectives, you can gather some information from external sources that can help you to decide which insurance companies you want to work with.

Consult with Colleagues

Your colleagues may be able to provide insight on which insurance companies they find easy to work with, or which ones they find to be more challenging to work with and why. Understanding your colleagues' experiences can inform your own choices, but always ask why! A colleague might have different ideas as to what makes an insurance company difficult to work with. For example, an insurance company may have online portals that your colleague finds difficult to use, but you consider yourself to be pretty tech savvy. At this point, you're gathering information to be able to make informed decisions. Here are a few questions to ask your colleagues when researching insurance companies:

- How has their overall experience been working with the insurance company?
- How long does the insurance company take to pay on average?
- Are claims submitted electronically or by paper?
- Does the insurance company offer direct deposit options?
- How readily accessible is their provider services department?
- What is the general range of reimbursement I can expect from the insurance company?
- Has it been easy to find patients locally with that insurance?

When discussing reimbursement rates, bear in mind that some insurance companies contractually require confidentiality regarding rates. Be respectful of your colleague's obligation to their contract if they are unable to provide exact reimbursement rates. A biller that has industry experience will also be able to give you good feedback on the range of payments that you can find.

Research Insurance Company Websites

You can learn quite a bit about what an experience working with an insurance company might be like by reviewing their website. You will want to look for provider resource areas, which may or may not be accessible to you as an uncredentialed provider, portals, blogs or news sections of the insurance company, and in general get a feel for how easily you are able to navigate the website and find information. The website can be considered an introduction to the relationship between you and an insurance company.

You will also want to research whether or not the insurance company is accepting new providers into their network. If you find out that an insurance company has a **closed network**, it means that the insurance company has reached the maximum number of providers that it will allow in its network, and any credentialing applications will be denied. If the network is closed for a particular insurance company, you will want to consider other options to credential with where the need for providers is greater, and the success of credentialing is more likely.

Evaluate for Market Dominance

You will want to get a good idea of the insurance landscape within your geographic area. Things to consider are major employers in the area and the insurance that they offer to their employees, whether there are any dominating insurances for the population that you are hoping to serve, and if there are any insurance companies headquartered near to your physical location. This can impact that number of patients that you are able to reach in your area.

To gain insight on the rates that the insurance company will pay you, you can look at the Medicare rates. A **fee schedule**, or a list of rates that an insurance company pays, is calculated using a fair bit of statistics on the Medicare rates. If you need to know a general number, without knowing the specifics, you can always look for the Medicare rates on the CMS website..

Fair warning this is a giant spreadsheet that includes every CPT code found in the handbook (which is thousands and thousands of codes). You will need to do a code specific search to find it, and the corresponding rate will give you a general sense of what the insurance company might pay you for services. Code 90837 for a 60 minute session is a good place to start, or a code that you know you will use most frequently.

Evaluate Whether the Insurance is Right For Your Practice

When it comes down to identifying your best insurance partners there are several internal factors that we encourage you to consider. When running a practice, it is important to acknowledge that some resources are limited, and some are plentiful. We believe that if you have enough self-awareness of your limitations and strengths you will be able to make the best decision for you, your practice, and your patients.

Time

Time is the one resource that you cannot buy or get back. When it comes to working with an insurance partner you have to evaluate whether the insurance partner is going to be a drain on your time or if they are going to enhance the time that you are spending building your practice. It will not come as a surprise to learn that not all insurance partners are created the same. Some of them are helpful and easy to work with and some are not.

Here are some questions that you can reflect on to help determine whether an insurance partner is a good fit for your practice for now:

- Does the insurance company seem to be efficient in answering questions through customer service support channels such as phone, email, or chat?
- Is the insurance partner going to be prepared to pay for claims on time?
- Does the insurance partner have systems and processes that I can understand and learn?
- Have my colleagues spoken well about the insurance partner?
- If I have staff, how much time will they spend with the insurance partner and will that time be profitable?

- Given my current to-do list, can I afford to place consistent time on my schedule with the insurance company?

This list is not exhaustive but it should give you a good sense as to whether an insurance partner will be the best fit for you.

Cost

There is always a cost to the decisions that we make in private practice. That cost could be in the form of time or money, but in this case we want to evaluate whether an insurance partner is going to be the best return on investment that you could make.

One way to evaluate the cost of partnering with an insurance company is to calculate the money you would make from seeing patients compared to what you are spending to become in-network with that insurance company. It is possible to spend time every month for several months in order to become in-network with an insurance company and you could pass on several thousand dollars of revenue in that process. Is that something that you are willing to do based on how much that insurance company will make for you?

Workload

Building a private practice from the ground up requires significant amounts of work, as you know. Are you able to add something else to your workload without burning out in the process? Taking insurance is not a one time deal. You have to commit to working with that insurance company day in and day out for years to come. You will have to adjust to administrative changes, rate changes, bureaucratic nonsense. Is your workload in a place that you can take on that burden?

Conversely, if you are in a place where you have an individual doing this work, is their workload able to adjust to accommodate another insurance partner? Be mindful that when you are adding an insurance partner you are adding recurring work to your schedule or someone else's schedule.

Morale

The last variable to consider when choosing an insurance partner is your morale. Are you in a stable place where adding more work doesn't seem like it is going to add unnecessary stress to your daily life? Does the idea of taking on an insurance company excite you or fill you with fear? If this decision is going to contribute to your feelings of regretting starting a practice in the first place we would encourage you to reflect on that more and decide on why this is a valuable endeavor for your practice.

On the other hand, if this strategic move is one that makes you excited to go to work and to be able to provide services to more and more patients then we would encourage you to go ahead with the process!

CHAPTER SUMMARY

The key to successfully taking advantage of insurance is planning effectively. If you are able to plan your insurance strategy and to gain clarity around the role that insurance plays in your practice you will be far more effective than someone that doesn't plan for taking insurance.

Follow-Up Actions to Take:

- Reflect on your clinical goals and objectives to see where your ideal patient may get their insurance from
- Do some math to determine how much your practice would make with each insurance mix if you collect 100% of your outstanding money
- Outline which Profitable Insurance Mix makes the most sense for your goals
- Ask some colleagues about which insurances they like working with and which ones they don't considering the questions above
- Evaluate each insurance company's website for clarity and ease of use
- Evaluate to see which insurance company or companies dominate the market where you are located
- Evaluate your time, cost, workload, and morale for taking insurance

Chapter 3:
HOW TO GET CREDENTIALED

Now that you have identified which insurance companies you want to work with to help you achieve your goals, you can begin the credentialing process. As we learned in Chapter 1, **Credentialing, or insurance credentialing,** is the process of applying and proving to the insurance company that a provider is qualified to see patients and be paid for services rendered. This process is slightly different for each insurance company, so as you begin your credentialing journey it will be important to approach each insurance company with a set plan to minimize the amount of mistakes that could be made.

DECIDE WHO IS COMPLETING YOUR CREDENTIALING

The first step is to decide who is actually going to do your credentialing. You can either complete the process yourself, or you can hire a professional to do your credentialing for you. In either case, a general understanding of the process is helpful so you can make educated choices throughout.

Credential Yourself

One of the biggest reasons providers choose to credential themselves, or have someone already within their organization handle the credentialing, is it saves on the startup costs of opening a private practice. You will need to weigh the financial cost against the time cost for you and your practice, as well as assess your own understanding of the credentialing process to decide whether or not you think you can manage credentialing on your own. We believe it is possible for providers to complete their own credentialing with time, attention to detail, and a good deal of patience.

Outsourcing

There are many reasons outsourcing may make sense for you and your practice. First and foremost, professional credentialers have experience. They are familiar with applications, terminology, and processes to make sure your credentialing is completed correctly. Secondly, credentialing applications take time to fill out. If you are feeling like your schedule is already at maximum capacity, you may want to consider outsourcing your credentialing process.

When choosing a credentialing partner, you will want to consider things such as price, the size of the organization doing credentialing, whether or not they have experience with mental health providers, and the general feeling you get from the company. We recommend identifying and interviewing a few candidates to make sure you make the right choice for you and your practice.

If you decide to outsource, you will still need to participate in the credentialing process. You need to be able to communicate your goals clearly to your credentialer, and understand the NPI and Tax ID information you would like to be credentialed with. You will also need to be able to read through drafts of applications and understand what is being submitted, and you will need to be mindful of signatures needed or information sent directly to you from the insurance company. The best way to stay in control of your practice is to be informed through your credentialing process, even if someone else is managing the time consuming paperwork.

WHAT YOU WILL NEED TO COMPLETE THE CREDENTIALING PROCESS

Regardless of who is doing your credentialing, you will need to collect a tremendous amount of information. Below we have included the information and documents you will need to gather before you start to complete applications. If you have all of this information organized beforehand, the process of credentialing will be much easier.

In order to make sure your time is used as efficiently as possible, we recommend creating a place to store all of this documentation so it is easily accessible. A digital file directory that is clear to you and allows you to gain access to this information quickly and easily is our best suggestion. You can also have a paper file, however you will likely need to provide digital copies of documents.

This list is long and can take some time to curate. To help you stay organized, we've formatted it as a checklist you can print out and mark each item as completed as you go. This list is a great starting point, but if you find yourself wondering "what's that?" to any of the items on this list, you may benefit from our professional service offerings.

Everything You Will Need to Complete Credentialing:

- Liability Insurance Certificate
- NPI Documentation from NPPES
- NPI Provider Application/Update Form (i.e. if you are joining a group)
- Copy of Social Security Card
- Copy of your Driver's License (front and back)
- Copy of your Professional License
- Set up your CAQH Account or Medversant account (be sure to securely store your login information)
- Decide your Provider Type (i.e. Clinical Social Worker)
- Copy of your Diploma (i.e both undergraduate and graduate)
- Addresses of your Undergraduate and Graduate Schools
- Copies of your CEU Certificates
- Names of Training Courses

- Name of the Practice you are joining or credentialing
  - Address of the Practice
  - Start Date at the Practice
  - Phone Coverage Hours
  - Tax ID of the Practice
  - Office Hours of the Practice
  - Names of the Partners at the Practice
  - Names of Colleagues that Cover Sessions in Your Absence
  - Name of the Office Manager at your Practice
  - Name of the Billing Contact at your Practice
  - Demographic Information of the Billing Contact at your Practice
- Payment and Remittance Information (i.e. Bank account information)
- Patient Limitations or Patients you Don't Take
- Disabled Accessibility Information
- List of Services Designated by CPT Code
- List of Treatment Modalities
- 4 Professional References
- Criminal and Civil History
- Login Password for PECOS
- Login Password for I/A (Information and Access, only applicable if applying to Medicare/Medicaid)
- Login to any Insurance Portal
- Copy of your EIN Documentation
- Copy of your LLC
- Copy of your Articles of Organization
- Copy of each completed application
- Steps to Apply for Each Panel

- The Credentialing Application for each insurance company you are applying to

COMPLETING THE CREDENTIALING PAPERWORK

Insurance applications are similar but not identical. They will ask for the same information in different ways and in different formats. Some of them still use paper applications, while others have adopted a more modern digital approach. We will provide general guidance below on completing credentialing paperwork, but if you are completing credentialing yourself and you run into any specific questions, your best course of action is to contact the insurance company directly for further guidance.

Your CAQH account or Medversant account will be important in this process. If you have not already done so, navigate to CAQH or Medversant or both and create your account. Having one or both of these accounts will enable you to fill out insurance applications quickly and provide insurance companies with the most accurate and up to date information. It will be important to ensure you attest to the accuracy of the data in CAQH or Medversant regularly. They will inform you when you need to update your information and it is important not to neglect that task.

Once you have all of the information from the list we gave you and your CAQH or Medversant account updated, then you are ready to begin filling out insurance applications. Remember, at this point you have done a lot of work to determine your insurance strategy and identify the insurance companies you are going to credential with. Now begins the fun process of getting credentialed.

Here are a couple of pointers as you go down the road of filling out insurance credentialing applications:

- Allow yourself plenty of time to fill out the applications. In some cases, the insurance companies will not allow you to save and return to the application. It is usually safe to budget 2-3 hours to fill out an application, but we recommend allowing yourself plenty of time to focus while you work on it, free of distraction. Any mistake made in the application will only serve to delay the acceptance of your application. You have done a lot of preparation to ensure that you have a smooth experience, don't ruin all that work by rushing through the application process.
- Be as detailed as possible. There are going to be times while filling out credentialing applications when you are not sure what to write or what to say. Take the time to think through what the insurance company is looking for and do your best to answer honestly. If you get stuck, contact the insurance company and ask for clarity. It would be better to be as detailed as possible on the front end than to fix a list of issues in 60 days when the application doesn't process and you have to start over.
- Concentrate on your strategy and the end goal of credentialing. There will be times you think, "Why am

I doing this?". Review the strategy you put together in Chapter 2 and that will help remind you exactly why you are doing this. Your strategy will also help you to make decisions through the credentialing process. For example, you may be asked if you are credentialing as a group or an individual. You will want to review your strategy to see if you want a group contract or to credential as a solo provider. Keeping your goals in mind will save you time and stress throughout the process.

- Edit and review the information before you submit the application. Almost all of the insurance applications will notify you when the information you have submitted is incorrect, but it is best when you can review and edit the information before submitting.

With over 400 insurance companies in the United States, each of them managing the insurance credentialing process slightly differently, it is impossible to provide step-by-step instructions to apply for each insurance company's panels in this book. In general, filling out insurance applications is all about detail and sticking to your predetermined strategy for your private practice. If you do those two things it will be much easier to credential you and your practice.

FOLLOWING UP ON CREDENTIALING APPLICATIONS

You have selected your preferred strategy, you have collected all of your information and you have submitted your application.

The next step is to follow up on your application with a specific and forensic process which allows you to be proactive in correcting any errors and be poised to take any next steps to being credentialed.

It is critical to make sure you are following up on your application as much as possible. Insurance companies are large corporations who do this all the time. While this may seem like it would make them experts with a flawless system, tasks within the insurance company are carried out by humans who can make mistakes, the same as anyone. The more thorough you are in the follow-up process, the more you can advocate for yourself in the event of any mistakes.

Here are steps you can take as you follow up to meet the specific and forensic criteria we mentioned earlier.

Confirm Receipt of Your Application

It is not uncommon for the insurance company to send you an email receipt stating your application has been received. There may also be a place within an online portal for the insurance company with a status bar showing where your application is in the process. Other times, you may need to call to verify your application has been received. We recommend calling and confirming with the insurance company even if you have received one of the digital confirmation messages. While confirming, you will want to ask if the insurance company has a reference number assigned to your application that you can use for future follow-ups.

Once your application has been received, it will move through the following stages:

- Initial Screening: The insurance company conducts an initial review to ensure that the application is complete and that all necessary documentation is included.
- Verification of Information or Primary Source Verification: Basic checks are performed to verify the accuracy of the information provided, including cross-referencing licenses and certifications with relevant boards and authorities.
- Committee Review: A credentialing committee, which often includes medical professionals and administrative staff, reviews the application and verification results.
- Decision and Notification: Based on the committee's review, the provider is either approved for credentialing or denied. Conditions or restrictions may be applied to the approval.
- Contracting: If the provider is approved, the insurance company may proceed with negotiating a contract outlining terms of participation in the network, reimbursement rates, and other conditions.

Create an Application Follow-Up Schedule

The next step in ensuring you are following-up consistently with the insurance company is to plan your next few follow-ups. Block out an hour or two to follow-up as insurance company phone wait times are usually long. We recommend following up after 15, 30, 45, 60, 90, 120, and 180 days. If 180 days have lapsed and your contract has not been processed, this is atypical and you will need to take additional action. In your calendar, schedule your follow-up days as you would an appointment. This is top priority and should be treated like a patient session or any other meeting you would not cancel, unless you have received a verbal update and a call reference number informing you that they will not give you an additional update for another 30 days. In this case, simply adjust your follow-up schedule to integrate this information.

Identify and Record Necessary Contact Information

After you have scheduled all of your follow-up days, make sure you have the correct contact information to obtain a status of your application. This phone number may have been provided when you submitted your application, but sometimes you may need to enquire for the best phone number. Once you determine the number you need to call, save that number on your follow-up spreadsheet so it is handy when you need it!

Follow The Call Script on Follow-Up Days

Every day you have scheduled a follow-up you are going to call the insurance company to obtain the status on your application. We suggest the following routine when following up:

a. Call the number you have saved
b. Get a representative on the phone as quickly and as politely as possible
c. Ask the name of the representative and document it on the follow-up spreadsheet
d. Give the representative the reference number for the application you submitted and ask the representative to clarify what stage of the process the application is in currently
e. Ask the representative what, if any, action you need to take or documentation you need to provide
f. Summarize the call to the representative
g. Ask the representative for the reference number of the call and document that on the follow-up spreadsheet
h. Document the summary in the follow-up spreadsheet
i. Confirm your next follow-up appointment according to the recommended Follow-Up Schedule and ask the representative if you can schedule another follow-up
j. If you need to submit additional documents or information as a result of the follow-up call, be sure to add these to your to-do list ASAP

You may be asking yourself, "That seems like overkill. Why can't I just ask and find out where my application is in the process?". We recommend using such a detailed process because you will be incredibly prepared should the insurance company make an error in the processing of your application. You will want objective evidence and documentation that you did everything you should have to push the application forward.

In the event that something goes wrong in the credentialing process, your follow-up log will be able to prove to a higher-up manager or the insurance commissioner that the insurance company did not hold up their end of the arrangement and is dragging their feet on processing your application. Insurance companies are also logging and recording your calls, so your log helps to tell your side of the story if necessary. If you have to ask for a manager they can compare your log against their internal call records to confirm your efforts, or identify their errors. In some cases, this has led to an application being expedited for processing.

Continue Follow-Ups Until You Receive Your Contract

You will want to continue the follow-up process for as long as it takes until you have received your contract. This may happen before you have completed the entire follow-up schedule you've created, which is great! You can remove additional follow ups from your calendar, and proceed to reviewing and signing your contract.

If 180 days have lapsed and you still have no recorded progress on your insurance application, you should use all of the information that you have logged through the follow-up process to escalate your case with a manager at the insurance company.

Following up on your insurance credentialing application is one of the best actions you can take when waiting for your application to be processed by the insurance company. Practice Solutions offers tools to help you manage the credentialing application process including a Credentialing Follow-Up Template as part of our Professional Services program. Once you have received a contract from the insurance company a whole new process begins where you will review the contract and fee schedule.

THE CONTRACTING PROCESS

The final stage in the credentialing process is receiving, reviewing, signing and returning your contract for processing. It is only after your signed contract has been received and processed at the insurance company that your credentialing process is complete and your in-network status official! Just receiving the contract can feel like overcoming a huge hurdle, but be careful not to relax too soon. You will want to make sure that you follow these next steps in their entirety before completing any counseling sessions or billing activity.

Receiving Your Contract

First, you will be notified by phone or by email that you have been accepted to the panel! This is certainly cause for celebration. This means the insurance company has reviewed all the documentation you sent over and they have verified that you are qualified to see patients. This does not mean that you can now send claims to the insurance company and expect payment for services rendered. If you send claims at this stage in the process they will be denied since you are still outside of their participating network until you return a signed contract.

A contract will most likely be sent electronically via email or insurance portal for your review following a notification, however it could also come by mail. If you don't receive a contract, be sure to check your spam folder. If it is not there, contact the insurance company directly to ask them when you should have received it, by what method, and to verify the address or email address that it was sent to. If necessary, request that they re-send the contract to you.

Reviewing Your Contract

You will want to review the contract thoroughly to make sure that it is satisfactory to you and your goals for your practice. Reviewing the contract should be done by you and by your practice's attorney. If you don't have an attorney, this is a great time to begin the process of hiring one or finding a trusted legal professional who is willing to represent you from time to time. This is not a contract that you should sign lightly. More than likely this is a contract that could result in millions of dollars paid to your practice over time. Make sure that the terms of the contract are agreeable to you.

Please note that we are not attorneys and do not provide legal advice to our clients and readers, however we have outlined some of the key aspects of your contract that you should be reviewing with your attorney. The following information should be included in your contract, and can inform procedures within your practice. If any of this information is not included in your contract, you will want to request it from the insurance company before signing.

Your Responsibilities

One of the first clauses in a contract with an insurance company will be a section outlining your responsibilities. This is an important clause because it tells you what the insurance company is expecting from you in the relationship moving forward. They will likely have multiple stipulations about confidentiality, claim submission requirements, and credentialing updates. Most of the time these contracts use standard language and formats but it is important that you read through this section carefully and understand what the insurance company is expecting from you in the relationship.

The Insurance Company's Responsibilities

In addition to your responsibilities, early in the contract will be a section outlining what you can come to expect from the insurance company in the relationship. Normally this section includes confidentiality, payment velocity, and any compliance requirements that the insurance company is required to adhere to according to local, state, or federal law.

Term and Termination

You will want to make note of how long your credentialing contract is valid for, and when you will need to re verify your credentials to keep your contract effective. You will also want to review options and procedure for termination should you ever decide to part ways with the insurance company. The last term length that you should look for in the contract has to do with rate negotiation; some insurance companies don't renegotiate rates until you have been on the panel for a certain amount of time, which would be noted in your contract if applicable.

Your contract may include an effective date, which is what the insurance company would have on record as the start date of your contract once processed. This effective date is not valid until the contract has been signed, returned, processed, and you have received your welcome letter. It is important to note your effective date, as you may be able to submit backdated claims or you may need to wait until the effective date for claims to be processed after you have received your welcome letter.

Compensation

Along with the contract you should receive a document called a **fee schedule**. The fee schedule outlines the **contracted rates or allowed amounts** that the insurance company has deemed acceptable as compensation for your services as an in-network provider; in other words, what you will be paid for services. This document is typically organized as a list of **CPT codes**, each with an assigned dollar amount or contracted rate, and it may list different amounts based on education level. Be sure to review the list according to your qualifications and license designation. This document is very important and we would go so far as to say that you should not sign the contract unless you have a valid and current fee schedule from the insurance company that you are attempting to be paneled with.

Not every insurance company pays the same, so it is important to know how your revenue will be impacted based on the type of insurance patient that you take on in your practice. Make sure that you keep these rates, and know that they are subject to change every year. It is a good practice to request an updated fee schedule annually since the insurance companies can change your rates and adjust the amount that you are paid. Your contract may also note the frequency and typical timing for rate changes or increases.

Your contract may designate that your Fee Schedule is proprietary information, meaning that it is not to be shared with other providers. If so, the insurance company will be very strict about giving the fee schedule to anyone other than the provider whose name is on the contract. When you are sharing fee information with a patient, avoid sharing the entire fee schedule. Tailor the information to your patient and only share the relevant CPT codes and associated costs to the patient's treatment. If the contract does not designate that your fee schedule is confidential, you can be more lenient. Fee schedules are proprietary information, and insurance companies will often be very strict about giving this document out to anyone other than the provider whose name is on the contract. Fee schedules are not to be shared among providers, and when you are sharing the fee information with a patient, avoid sharing the entire fee schedule. Tailor the information to your patient and only share the relevant CPT codes and associated costs to the patient's treatment.

The insurance fee schedule has many uses throughout the billing process, and we will discuss more about it as we get into the details of each stage of revenue cycle management.

Timely Filing

Timely filing is the amount of time that a provider has from the date of service to submit a claim to the insurance company to ensure that the insurance company will pay the claim. If the provider does not submit claims to the insurance company within timely filing limits the insurance company will deny the claim and the provider will not be paid for those services. Each insurance company has a different timely filing limit, and denials for submitting claims outside of the timely filing limit are final and cannot be appealed.

Timely filing is also the amount of time that a provider has to submit an appeal on any denial that was received. For some insurance companies you have to keep in mind that the timely filing limit for the initial service and the timely filing limit for an appeal may actually be different. If you are receiving a lot of denials this is something that will need to be addressed quickly in order to see if you have an opportunity for payment.

Submitting Claims

A simple but overlooked part of the contract is where to submit claims once you are contracted and paneled with the insurance company. In the digital age we now send most claims electronically, and some insurance companies even require digital claim submission, but there is not one unified holding place for claims. Each clearinghouse and each insurance company has a slightly different system to identify where claims should go. In this section of the contract you are looking for something called the **submitter ID**. The submitter ID is the numerical identification number that you will use in your electronic health record system to send claims and make sure they arrive at the appropriate destination.

Furthermore the contract should give you a physical address to send claims and correspondence, which may be different from the overall address of the insurance company. You will need to save this address to send denial information, appeal information, clinical information, and occasionally a physical claim form.

Credentialing Identifiers

Finally, double check your name, your practice's name, your address, your contact information, the NPI and tax ID, your education level, and the organization type that is listed in the contract. This is what you will use to identify yourself to the insurance company on future claims, so make sure that it is correct according to all of your credentialing application documents. If any of your identifying information is incorrect, contact the insurance company to change the information on the contract before signing.

Signing and Returning

After you have reviewed the contract you will sign and return the contract for processing. Make sure to follow any instructions provided as to how the contract needs to be signed and returned, such as whether or not an e signature is acceptable, whether a notary is required or if the contract needs to be returned by mail or email.

After you have signed and returned the contract for processing, billing claims still will not be processed at the in-network level. You must wait for notification from the insurance company via a welcome letter in order to begin billing claims. If you have an effective date for your In Network status, you may begin seeing patients as of that date, but wait for your welcome letter before submitting the associated claims.

Confirmation of Contract Processing

The final stage of the credentialing process is to receive a welcome letter confirming that your contract has been processed. Once you have received your welcome letter you are credentialed as an in-network provider at that insurance company and can begin billing claims for that insurance. This is a sizable accomplishment! You can now be paid by the insurance company for services that you provide to your patients.

Your Insurance Fee Schedule or Contracted Rates

The fee schedule is sometimes sent as part of the contract with the insurance company, however it could also be a separate document. You will have a different fee schedule for every insurance company that you are credentialed with.

There are some insurance companies that don't provide a fee schedule when you are in the credentialing process and they offer fee schedules only on request. You will want to request a copy of the fee schedule. Otherwise, you can submit claims and see how the claim processes and pays and record that information to develop your own fee schedule. We don't recommend this option as a good option because if the insurance company makes a mistake on the first payment you could go months and even years without fair compensation.

The fee schedule is useful in several of the following stages of revenue cycle management, including charge capture, claim submission, and payment posting. As a practice owner, you can use the information on your fee schedule to project revenue. You can use the numbers on a fee schedule to create projections of income in your practice, or you can set goals for yourself on the average number of sessions you would need to complete in a week to meet a specific level of income.

CHAPTER SUMMARY

Using the list you created in Chapter 2 of insurance companies you want to work with to help you achieve your goals, you can begin the credentialing process. This process is slightly different for each insurance company, so as you begin your credentialing journey it will be important to approach each insurance company with a set plan to minimize the amount of mistakes that could be made. You should now have a comprehensive view of the credentialing process and how you would like to move through that process. Here are some actionable steps to take to move your practice to the next level.

Follow-Up Actions to Take

- Decide who will be doing your credentialing
- Use our checklist to gather all of the relevant documentation to successfully credential with insurance
- Save all of your documentation in an easily accessible folder
- Decide on an insurance company to credential with
- Contact the insurance company to obtain the application or access to the application
- Fill in the application
- Review the application
- Submit and follow-up on the application keeping notes along the way
- Receive, Review, and Sign Contract
- Receive Welcome Letter confirming "In Network" status
- Understand the claim submission process for when you are ready to submit claims

Chapter 4:
PREPARATION FOR BILLING

At this stage, you have learned the basics of billing and credentialing, and how the two processes are closely related. You also have a defined strategy for accepting insurance, and know how to get credentialed to execute your strategy. You have developed a solid foundation for your practice's success in insurance billing! In this chapter we are going to talk about how you can best prepare you, your practice, your team, and your patients for billing insurance. We believe one of the keys to successful billing lies in preparedness, allowing you to follow a pre-designed process rather than figuring things out as you go. This should ultimately yield fewer mistakes and headaches in billing. One of the first things you can do to prepare for billing is to celebrate your success so far. You have done a lot of preparation already and you should celebrate that success!

After you are done celebrating we will discuss your next steps, including selecting an electronic health record system, setting up and utilizing online portals, and establishing the capability to send electronic claims and receive electronic payment.

SELECTING AN EHR

As we defined in Chapter 1, EHR stands for an Electronic Health Record system, and is a tool designed for healthcare providers to store patient data, schedule appointments, complete progress notes, and generate and submit claims. In the current age of technology, an EHR is practically non-negotiable. Not only do some insurance companies require electronic claim submission, but your patients have come to expect the convenience and security of a provider utilizing an electronic system. Your EHR is going to be something that you interact with on a daily basis, so you should spend time selecting the best EHR for you and your practice. When selecting an EHR, you should consider the following factors.

HIPAA Compliance/Security

Many of the current headlines have featured cyber attacks against government authorities or businesses, notably the attack against the clearinghouse Change Healthcare. Healthcare is a prime target for hackers or cyber-criminals. Because of this reality, it is the duty of the biller and the practitioner to maintain and use software that will protect your patient's health information.

When choosing an EHR, be sure to talk to a company representative about their HIPAA compliance program and their security measures to protect against any kind of cyber attack. When discerning who has the better security program, you can look at the staff. If the management is hiring experienced IT professionals, it is a good indicator that they are preparing for the security of health information. You may also want to investigate the size and number of the clearinghouse(s) that the EHR works with. More options for clearinghouses protects against any outages, and the size of the clearinghouse can give you an indication of their processing volume.

User Experience

An EHR ought to be user-friendly. Many times, therapists get into an EHR and all they see is a database-type interface that is unreadable. Fortunately, there are EHRs that exist where even the least technologically savvy practitioner can navigate with ease. Because your cash-flow is often tied to the EHR used, the need for the software to be user-friendly is a must.

Along with being user friendly, the ability to customize the fields or the needed reports is a wonderful thing. It's important to shop around for the right software. Make a list of all the patient demographic fields that you hope to have in a software and search for EHR options with those list items in mind. For example: marital status, number of sessions, employer, etc. You will want to find a software that helps you track the information that will equip you to best serve your patients.

Features

The basic features of an EHR should include:

- Payer Management
- Provider Management

- EDI (claim) submission
- ERA receiving
- Reports on outstanding money from patients and insurance
- Facesheets (patient demographic information)
- Treatment planning
- Note taking

Most EHRs will have many more features, but these are the basics. If your EHR is missing any of these, it is not worth your time.

Customer Service

Customer service is an incredibly important facet of choosing an EHR. You will want a knowledgeable, responsive, and helpful customer service department to support your use of the software. The worst case scenario is choosing an EHR that has bad customer service that ends up costing you time, energy, and money or that can't help you when you need help most.

Cost

One of the biggest factors in using an EHR is the cost. Some EHRs have a flat-fee every month, some have a variable fee every month, and some have a one time purchase fee. There are several factors that go into cost, but generally you can spend between $20.00 a month or even $500.00 a month on an EHR depending on the size of your practice and your EHRs capabilities. This is yet another reason why making that "must-haves" list for your software is so vital. You might be able to save yourself money by determining from the beginning that you don't need the 25 special features offered by the $500/month software and land on a more reasonable price point.

What you want to spend depends on the size and needs of your practice. Most practices don't want to expend the capital for the most expensive EHRs, but there are some cost-effective solutions out there even for group practices.

Common EHRs To Start Looking Into for Mental Health Practitioners

*SimplePractice
Theranest
TherapyAppointment
*TherapyNotes

*Indicates compatibility with Practice Solutions Billing Services

SETTING UP ONLINE INSURANCE PORTALS

Insurance portals are a great free online tool for mental healthcare providers who are billing insurance. Through these portals, you can establish secure HIPAA compliant connections to payers so you can perform eligibility and benefit checks for your patients, submit claims, receive ERAs, and more. Portals are at the forefront of advancing technology in the healthcare industry. If you are a provider accepting insurance, we recommend setting up an account in the portal for each insurance company you are credentialed with, or following each insurance company's social accounts so that you can stay up to date on advancements made in the industry.

Who Operates these portals?

Sometimes portals are operated by a third party entity that serves as a bridge between healthcare providers and insurance providers, but sometimes they are operated by the insurance company themselves. The most common third party portal is called Availity. Many different insurance companies utilize Availity as their portal system, making all insurances utilizing Availity accessible with a single login. We have even seen insurance companies with their own established portals switching to or adding in access through Availity due to its user friendly interface and wide ranging capabilities. There are still many insurance companies operating their own portals as well, and each individual portal will function a little differently. The ultimate goal of portals is to eliminate the gap between insurance companies and providers by providing real time information regarding claim status, eligibility, and payment.

Who Should Have an Insurance Portal?

If you are a provider who is accepting insurance, we recommend that you set up an account with every insurance portal offered! In today's insurance landscape, there are very few insurance companies who do not offer some form of online portal.

By setting up an account with an insurance portal you get industry news and updates from the company sent directly to you. If you're intimidated by learning another portal, they have plenty of tutorials and a large support team that can help you learn and make the most of the platform. Our best recommendation is to keep a log of all of your portals and the login information for each. You will want to store these logins safely as they can provide access to claims and patient data. We recommend using online password storage tools that are HIPAA compliant to manage these logins.

What Can I Do With My Insurance Portals?

Online portals provide access to information that is pertinent to the stages of revenue cycle management that we learned about in Chapter 1. Without the online portals, you may find yourself spending unnecessary hours on hold with the insurance company. Here are some of the functions that are accessible through most online portals:

Perform Eligibility and Benefit Checks

You can use portals to check eligibility and benefits for your patients in advance of their session with you during the pre-registration phase of revenue cycle management. This allows you to be informed and prepared to explain what a patient will owe you for the session, and what will be covered by insurance.

View Fee Schedule Information

As a credentialed provider, it is possible that your fee schedule may be accessible through an online portal, and you could check there before calling the insurance company to request the fee schedule. If fee schedule information is available through the online portal for an insurance company, it is good practice to review the fee schedule annually for any changes in reimbursement rates so that you can adjust coinsurances and claim rates accordingly.

Claim Submission

You can submit claims through portals to various insurance companies. Claims can either be submitted directly in the portal, or by establishing an EDI connection between the portals and your EHR. This connection allows claims to be submitted securely and HIPAA compliant through digital channels.

Check Claim Status

Follow-ups on claims in portals are typically easy! You can view the Claim Status section of the portal and learn where each claim is at in the process.

Receive ERA

Portals allow you to set up ERA delivery directly to your EHR, or you can view ERAs in the portal. This allows you to see how claims were processed and paid, or learn more information about why a claim was denied.

View Payment Status

Through portals you can check the status of a claim payment. You can get a clear picture of funds that will be coming into your practice.

Sign Up for EFT Payment

EFT, or electronic funds transfer, is a method of direct deposit from the insurance company for claim payouts. If you have not yet signed up for electronic payment by providing your bank account and routing numbers, you can often do so through portals! Say goodbye to waiting for checks through the mail and hello to easy direct deposit!

SETTING UP ELECTRONIC CLAIM SUBMISSION AND REMITTANCE

Once you have established your EHR system and you have created any necessary online portals, you can begin the enrollment process of establishing electronic claim submission and remittance for billing purposes. This allows you to save time in the revenue cycle management process.

EDI and ERA Enrollment: What are they?

EDI is the term used to describe electronic claim submission, and **EDI Enrollment** is the process of establishing a secure connection between your EHR and the insurance company. Applying for EDI involves connecting your EHR system to a clearinghouse whose role is to pass on digital claim submissions from your EHR to the insurance company. The clearinghouse serves a few different purposes, namely scrubbing claims for potential errors, and routing claims to insurance companies through secure and HIPAA compliant channels. Applying for EDI allows you to submit claims electronically as an ANSI-X12-837 file, rather than the traditional paper method of the CMS-1500 form. This is why you may see the term 837 during the application process for EDI, referring to the electronic file type.

ERA Enrollment makes it so that upon processing of claims, an ERA file is transmitted electronically from the insurance company through the clearinghouse to your EHR. This file contains information about how much was paid, which claims were paid, and which claims were denied, if any. This file may be referred to as an 835, which again is derived from the name of the file type.

Tips for Setting Up EDI and ERA

The process for EDI and ERA enrollment can differ based on the EHR you are using, as well as the insurance company that you are intending to submit claims to. A good place to start would be to review our list of documents and information necessary for getting credentialed, outlined in Chapter 3. Many of these identifiers will be needed in setting up EDI. Next, check with your EHR and see if they have instructions to help you in setting up the EDI connection with their preferred clearinghouse for a specific payer. Some payers will have automatic enrollment through an EHR that does not require paperwork, or you may need to fill out paperwork to submit to the clearinghouse, as well as to the insurance company. There may also be an online enrollment process that the insurance company may be able to help walk you through.

There are three entities involved in EDI: your EHR company, the clearinghouse, and the insurance company. Each of them likely has a point of contact for EDI, and it may be helpful to contact each entity if you are having trouble with getting EDI setup. You can also refer to each of their websites for information related to EDI setup.

When applying for ERA , it is important to make sure that the information submitted is the same as what was submitted for EDI, which should be the same information as what you credentialed with. Making sure that all of the information matches up is the most important!

Again, check with your EHR for specific instructions on how to apply for ERA, as they may have paperwork available for you to complete with some further instructions on where to send it.

For both EDI and ERA you may also need an identifier for the EHR system that you work with. You will need to know which clearinghouse your EHR works with, which may also have an assigned code or identifier, and lastly you will need to know the **Payer ID** of the insurance company that the clearinghouse has assigned to that payer.

Getting these connections set up can be daunting, but there are many people who are able to support you in the process! Communicating with a representative from your EHR is a great place to start, as they can tell you which clearinghouse you should be working with. Getting in touch with the EDI/ERA department of the insurance company is also helpful, as they can explain any portals or processes specific to them that may be required for the enrollment. Lastly, the clearinghouse itself is a great contact to have, as they can provide you with status updates of your enrollment, or they may be able to identify any issues with the enrollment.

Practice Solutions includes EDI and ERA setup as part of our billing service. We believe firmly in the impact of digital submission on the impact of revenue cycle management. In some cases, digital submission is actually required by the insurance company, and in all other cases digital submission removes a lot of the waiting time from revenue cycle management. You are no longer waiting for paper claims to be mailed, no longer waiting for paper explanations of benefits, and no longer waiting for paper checks. You still have to allow for claim processing time, but the use of digital tools is the most efficient for billing. We know it's confusing- that's why we manage the EDI and ERA setup for all of our billing clients.

CHAPTER SUMMARY

In this chapter you have learned the ins and outs of EHR selection, portal creation, and the billing process from a high-level. You are now equipped with all the information you will need to understand the lifecycle of a claim and have the confidence to know you will be paid for services that you render in your private practice. You should know how you will receive payment and record the details of that payment within your EHR system. Here are some actions we recommend taking now that you are equipped with the proper information to prepare for billing.

Follow-Up Actions to Take

- Make your list of ideal features in an EHR

- Research 3-5 EHR systems that you are interested in working with
- Detail the cost, capabilities, and functionality of those systems
- Decide and commit to a particular system
- Learn and familiarize yourself with the EHR system
- Establish portals with the insurance companies you are credentialed with
- Save the login information
- Familiarize yourself with those portals
- Ensure payment from the insurance company is being directed at the right location
- Establish any EDI and ERA connections that you can within your EHR

Chapter 5:
ESTABLISHING PATIENT RELATIONSHIPS

Once all of that preparation work has been completed, you will be in the best position to start accepting patients as an in-network provider and getting paid for your therapy sessions! You will first need to attract new patients to your practice. Then you will need to complete the first two stages of revenue cycle management. You must start developing the relationship with the patient in the pre-registration phase, collecting necessary information and scheduling an appointment, then you will need to complete the registration phase when your patient is in your office for their appointment, finalizing any patient details and collecting patient identification to keep on file.

CREATE YOUR PATIENT PAPERWORK DOCUMENTS

There are four documents that you will want to have established before you are truly ready to take on a patient. You can either create these documents yourself, or find a resource that has document templates available for purchase. These include your HIPAA Consent Form, your Patient Intake Paperwork which collects relevant demographic information, your practice's

Financial Policy and finally a Payment Collection Form. Your financial policy should address your policy to keep payment information on file, expectations for payment timing, session cancellation fees, patient responsibility following an E&B check, your standard rates and any sliding scale or financial hardship policies you may have. You may also want to consider having a Release of Information form for patients to authorize information to be shared with other individuals.

HOW TO ACQUIRE PATIENTS

Acquiring patients is not our area of expertise, however we have worked with enough providers to provide some general tips on ways that you can attract patients to your practice. Afterall, without patients, there is no insurance billing to complete! Consider these tips as a starting point, but we recommend doing some further research on resources that can help you to market your practice and reach the patients that will help you achieve your mission. The goal setting that you did in Chapter 2 can serve as a guidepost for your marketing decisions.

Utilize Resources from Your Insurance Partners

One of the benefits of getting credentialed is that the insurance company will list you as an in-network provider on their registry. Patients with that insurance can find you through the insurance company website. Look for a place where you can edit your listing and add some personalization to your provider profile on the insurance company's registry so that potential patients can learn more about you and your practice. A great first step would be to add a photo and a short description.

Expand Your Online Presence

Expanding your online presence is a great way to help boost your business, leading to increased revenue for your billing department to collect. Think about the last time you needed to find a healthcare provider- the first thing you did was likely an internet search. Most people are searching online and selecting healthcare providers based on their online presence, so you need to have a website that reflects your brand, your mission, and attracts patients that you want to work with. You probably have a website for your practice, but when was the last time you updated it? If it's been a while, you should fix that. Updating your site regularly with high quality content shows search engines that you are more likely to be a relevant business to searchers and can impact where you show up on search engine results.

Many providers utilize Psychology Today's online directory to list their practice in addition to their own website. Through the directory patients can search for providers in their area, and you can create a short bio that helps patients find the care that they are looking for. This is a great option to help you build your client base.

Build Customer Convenience into Your Practice

You can organically create a customer experience that makes a patient inclined to leave a positive review. Convenience matters most to patients, which is why EHR selection that offers convenient patient portals and online scheduling is an important step in preparation. You might also consider adding office hours outside of normal business hours. Make it easy for them to choose your clinic by making it the most convenient one to go to.

Making Billing Convenient
Making billing as convenient as possible for patients can help improve their overall experience and make it easier for your business to collect the money it is due. Offering personalized payment solutions can make billing more convenient for customers and improve your billing department's ability to collect money.

Make Smart Hiring Choices
Who you hire to handle your billing can make a huge difference in the experience your patients have with your practice. Billing is a pain point for medical practices in general. Having competent employees who understand the ins and outs of medical billing and excel at customer service can help with that. You should see fewer mistakes and improved patient satisfaction, especially in terms of the billing process, if you have an excellent billing team.

RCM STAGE 1: PRE-REGISTRATION

We learned in Chapter 1 that Pre-Registration occurs before your patient is in your office- they have likely submitted an online contact form, or have called your office to learn more about scheduling an appointment with you. It is at this time that you will want to start collecting information from your potential patient to determine if this will be a beneficial relationship between you and the patient. This is also a great opportunity to inform your patient of everything that they should bring and be prepared with when they come into your office for an appointment.

You will have information to collect from a therapeutic perspective, and those points should be discussed before any of the administrative and billing information is collected to help establish a positive patient relationship. From a billing perspective, the following information should be collected from your patient during the pre-registration process:

- Patient Full Legal Name
- Name of the Subscriber and Relationship to the Insured
- Patient Date of Birth and Date of Birth of the Subscriber
- Subscriber SSN
- Patient Address
- Name of **Insurance Provider**
- **Secondary Insurance Information** (If Applicable)
- Copy of the Patient's **Insurance Card** (front and back)
- Copy of the Patient's Driver's License or ID

- Copy of the Subscriber's Driver's License or ID (if different from the Patient)
- Treatment the patient is seeking
- Signed **HIPAA Consent Form**
- Signed **Financial Policy**
- Signed **Payment Information Form**

Patient Full Legal Name
Make sure that the name of the patient that you have in your system matches the patient's name that is listed on the insurance card. Be sure to confirm the proper spelling of the patient's name as it would appear in the insurance system.

Name of the Subscriber and Relationship to Insured
The subscriber is the primary beneficiary of the insurance policy. If your patient is on a parent or spouse's insurance plan, make sure to get the parent or spouses full name as well with proper spelling because they are the subscriber. Identify the relationship of the insurance plan holder to your patient (ie; father, mother, spouse, etc.)

Patient Date of Birth and Date of Birth of Subscriber
You will need the date of birth of your patient, as well as the date of birth of the subscriber. Many times this is the patient, however it could also be the date of birth of a parent, spouse, or legal guardian.

Subscriber SSN

You will need the social security number of the subscriber for claim submission.

Patient Address

Make sure that you have an updated address for your patient and that you collect all necessary information.

Name of Insurance Provider

The insurance card should include the name of the insurance company that claims should be sent to. Make sure that you properly identify the insurance company so that claims are submitted to the proper place. The back of the insurance card should also have an address for the insurance company that claims should be directed to.

Secondary Insurance Information (If Applicable)

Confirm with your patient or your patient's parents whether they have a secondary insurance plan. If the patient is covered under two different insurance plans, you will need to ask the patient which is primary and which is secondary so that claims can be submitted properly according to the Coordination of Benefits. If the patient does have a secondary insurance plan, you will need the name of the secondary insurance provider, and the information for the subscriber of this insurance plan including full name, date of birth, and social security number.

Copy of the Front and Back of the Patient's Insurance Card

Most of the information that you need to collect can be found on the patient's insurance card. If you collect the information from the patient as well as collect a copy of their actual card, it can be a helpful reference if you run into claim submission issues later on. You will be able to reference the exact card that was provided to you, look for any discrepancies, and easily check whether or not a patient has a new insurance card on returning visits by comparing their current card to the card you have on file. If you can, have your patient send you a copy of the front and back of their insurance card digitally. Be sure to make a copy of both the front and back of the card.

Copy of the Patient and Subscriber's Driver's License or ID

A copy of the driver's license or ID can help to make sure that you have the proper spelling of the patient or subscriber's name, and that you have their full legal name. If the patient and subscriber are two different people, you should collect identification from both.

Treatment the Patient is Seeking

You will want to be sure that you are able to provide the patient with the treatment that they need. You will also want to make sure that you schedule the appropriate amount of time and know the billing codes associated with the session and treatment that you schedule.

Signed HIPAA Consent Form

You should have all patients sign a HIPAA Consent Form in order to submit a claim for their session. This form should inform the patient that their protected health information may be shared with a third party clearinghouse in order for an insurance claim to process.

A provider's office may collect the copy of the patient's insurance card and the HIPAA consent form digitally in this stage. In fact, it is preferable in many circumstances because a digital collection of this material translates to less office hours needed on the day of the session. Collecting this information as quickly in the process as possible will benefit you later in the billing process. If you are unable to obtain these documents digitally, you can always collect them during stage 2, the registration phase.

Signed Financial Policy

The financial policy is another document that you can either collect in pre-registration if you have the capability to do so digitally, or you can wait until the registration phase when the patient is in your office.

Signed Payment Information Form

The payment information form should collect your patient's credit card number, name on the credit card, security code, and address. This can be used to charge the patient's card for any payments that they owe following a session. Again, if you are unable to collect this form digitally during pre-registration you can collect the information when the patient is in your office for the registration phase.

The last step of the pre-registration process is completing an **eligibility and benefits check** for your patient by contacting the patient's insurance provider to verify their benefits and coverage for your services. In Chapter 6, we will discuss exactly how to complete an eligibility and benefits check. If any portion of the patient information that you have collected is incorrect, an eligibility and benefits check will not be able to be performed until the correct information has been obtained. Completing an eligibility and benefits check before your patient comes into a session is always preferable, but you may run into situations where eligibility cannot be checked until the registration phase. Whenever you can, make sure that eligibility is checked during pre-registration.

You will want to establish a pre-registration process that makes the most sense for both your business and your patients. It is important to consider what the patient's experience will be when working with you or your team, as well as how each piece of information that is gathered helps you to submit clean claims and receive payment from the insurance company if this person becomes a patient.

From a customer experience standpoint, consider the following questions when designing your pre-registration process:

- Who within your office completes pre-registration? Do you have an admin who does this, or are you completing the pre-registration process?

- What online tools are you utilizing to aid in the pre-registration process, such as contact submission forms, patient portals, or HIPAA compliant email services?
- What is the script that you or your office staff is going to use to greet potential patients or new patients?
- What information makes the most sense to gather at this point, both for billing and for treatment of your patient?
- How does the patient schedule an appointment with you or any other therapist in your office?
- If you are a group practice, how does your administrator know which patient is a good fit for a specific therapist?

Make sure that as you design your process you document it thoroughly in a way that makes it easy to communicate with your team, an admin, or even for yourself to reference back to as your practice is established.

RCM STAGE 2: REGISTRATION OR PATIENT INTAKE PROCESS

When a patient is physically present in your office, it can be easier to collect and verify some of the information that you need for billing purposes. It also allows you to set the tone in person for the experience that your patient can expect while working with you. You want to make sure that you create an environment that is comfortable for your patient while also achieving the necessary goals that will make insurance billing run smoothly.

This step in the process answers questions like:

- What forms do they need to sign?
- Where do they fill out forms?
- How does that information become entered or verified in your **EHR system**?
- Do you have a copy of the necessary insurance card and IDs?

In many practices, this function is completed by an office administrator or front desk manager. If you do not yet have someone fulfilling this role in your office, you may be the one completing these tasks until you are ready to hire someone. Regardless of who is completing the registration phase, you need to have a clearly defined workflow and make sure that this process operates with an extremely high level of accuracy and precision. Any wiggle room in this process opens the possibility for errors in the claim submission process later on.

In the registration process, you should verify the following with your patient in-office:

- You have a signed HIPAA consent form on file for the patient
- You have reviewed your office's Financial Policy with the patient and collected a signed copy acknowledging the terms
- You have payment information to be kept on file for charging the patient

- You have a copy of the front and back of the patient's current insurance card(s)
- All information that you collected in the pre-registration phase is correct, and you have collected any necessary information that was previously missed
  - Patient Full Legal Name
  - Full Legal Name of the Subscriber and Relationship to the Insured
  - Patient Date of Birth and Date of Birth of the Subscriber
  - Subscriber SSN
  - Patient Address
  - Name of **Insurance Provider** with their ID # and Group #
  - Name of **Secondary Insurance Provider** (If Applicable) with their ID # and Group #
- All information has been entered into your EHR system and is spelled correctly
- Whether or not an eligibility and benefit check has been completed. If it has not, you will need to do so during this phase with the expectation that the patient will be charged for services before leaving the office (even if this happens at the end of the therapy session). If you are the one completing both the administrative and therapeutic functions in the office, you will want a very thorough pre-registration process so you can guarantee that you are paid for services during that first session.
  - Collecting patient credit card information on an authorization form ensures you are able to process

the correct patient payment even if they leave before you are unable to obtain benefit information.

Many providers choose to use tools such as online portals that allow patients to input this information online, where it can be directly translated into an EHR system. Check whether your chosen EHR has something like this available that you can utilize in your practice. You can also collect this information using fillable electronic documents or using paper documents that the patient completes while in the office, and then manually transfer information into your EHR. In either case, we recommend that you are always double checking the information entered into your EHR against the insurance card to prevent billing errors which would result in non-payment. The more detailed you are during the registration process, the easier it will be for you to submit claims and get paid.

CHAPTER SUMMARY

From this chapter you should have a general idea around how you are planning to acquire patients in your private practice. You must start developing the relationship with the patient in the pre-registration phase, collecting necessary information and scheduling an appointment, then you will need to complete the registration phase when your patient is in your office for their appointment, finalizing any patient details and collecting patient identification to keep on file.

You have learned how critical this stage of the billing process is and why it is important for the health of your practice to be disciplined in this process. The ease of billing will largely depend on how well you are organized in this stage of private practice. Here are some tips to help you move this process forward in your private practice:

Follow-Up Actions to Take

- Develop a strategy for how you will acquire patients
- As you execute your strategy decide on metrics to help you evaluate how successful you are
- Make changes as needed to your patient acquisition strategy
- Make pre-registration and registration checklists to follow for collecting patient information using the lists in each section above
- Develop or buy the necessary paperwork to capture all the information you need from your patients
- Develop a process for getting the patient paperwork into the EHR system
- Continually improve your internal processes so the patient has the easiest experience with your practice

Chapter 6:
ELIGIBILITY AND BENEFIT CHECKS

As we have mentioned before, eligibility and benefits checks allow you to confirm with the insurance company that your patient has an active insurance plan, whether or not your services are covered by the patient's plan, and details about what the patient will owe you for your services or what the insurance company will cover. This will ideally be completed during the pre-registration phase of revenue cycle management, but can be done in the registration phase if necessary. In this section, we will provide a deeper definition of eligibility and benefits, teach you the steps you can use to perform an eligibility and benefit check, and how to understand the information you receive from an eligibility and benefit check.

THE DIFFERENCE BETWEEN ELIGIBILITY AND BENEFITS

Eligibility and benefits may seem similar and are often used as a single term, but they have distinct differences that are important to understand. In this section, we'll explore the difference between eligibility and benefits, verification of benefits, plan year, deductible, and insurance, and how they impact your practice.

Eligibility refers to whether a patient is covered by an insurance plan. It determines if a patient has a valid insurance policy that can be used to pay for mental health services. Eligibility is usually determined by factors such as employment status, age, relationship to the policyholder, and enrollment in a specific insurance plan. It's essential to verify a patient's eligibility before providing any services to ensure that they are covered and that you will be reimbursed for your services.

On the other hand, **benefits** refer to the specific coverage under an insurance plan. This includes the amount that is reimbursable by the insurance company for this type of service. Benefits can vary greatly depending on the insurance plan and may include services such as therapy sessions, medication management, and psychiatric evaluations. Benefits may also have limitations, such as a maximum number of sessions allowed per year or restrictions on certain types of therapy. It's crucial to understand the specific benefits of each patient's insurance plan to provide accurate information about their coverage and potential out-of-pocket costs.

Verification of benefits or performing an **Eligibility and Benefits Check** is the process of confirming the details of a patient's insurance coverage. This typically involves contacting the insurance company directly or using an online portal to check the patient's eligibility and benefits. Verification of benefits is an essential step to ensure that you have accurate information about the patient's coverage, including their **deductibles, copayments**, and any other **out-of-pocket expenses**. It helps you and your patients understand the financial aspects of their mental health care and make informed decisions about their treatment. We recommend eligibility and benefit checks to be completed during the pre-registration phase because this ensures that when the patient is in your office during the registration phase, you are able to collect any payments owed immediately.

Understanding the plan year is also crucial when dealing with insurance. An **insurance plan year** is the specific time period during which an insurance plan's benefits are calculated. It typically lasts for 12 months, although it may not align with the calendar year. At the beginning of each plan year, the insurance plan resets, and deductibles, copayments, and out-of-pocket maximums may start over. It's important to be aware of the timing of the plan year, whether it resets on January 1 with the calendar year or another specified date, as it can impact the patient's out-of-pocket expenses and coverage limitations.

HOW TO DO AN E&B CHECK

All of the information that is collected in the pre-registration and registration phases will be necessary for you to complete an eligibility and benefit check. In this section, we will cover what you should be prepared with before you call the insurance company, and all of the information that you should collect when you have an insurance representative on the phone.

Eligibility and Benefit checks are important to avoid late or incorrect payments from patients. They can greatly increase a practice's cash flow, but they are time consuming. By being prepared and staying patient, these can go smoothly.

What to Know Before You Call the Insurance Company

Have the Correct Contact Information

You will want to refer to the patient's insurance card. Confirm the insurance provider on the front of the card, and refer to the phone number provided on the back of the insurance card. There may be multiple phone numbers, and if so look for a phone number that is specified for providers to check eligibility and benefits. This is the number that you will need to call to get the most accurate information the fastest. If using a portal, make sure that you have the correct portal information for the patient's insurance.

We recommend creating a list of each insurance payer that you are in-network with and the best method to retrieve E&B information. This can include portal login information, phone numbers, contact names, and additional instructions for performing E&B checks.

Be Prepared with Your Patient Information

When checking eligibility and benefits, the phone or portal system is going to require some standard information. Be sure you have all of the information collected during pre-registration including the patient's name, date of birth, address, and insurance card. Also, make sure you have your NPI or tax ID along with the address where services will be rendered. Don't waste time searching for this information while on the phone, have it pulled up in your EHR and readily available.

Block Out Time

You can end up on hold with the insurance company for a long time when checking eligibility. Block out at least an hour in your calendar, and be prepared with something that you can work on while you are on hold. Not all calls will take an hour, but it is better to have blocked out the time and get the information you need than to only block out 5 minutes and be unsuccessful. Keep in mind that you will likely only need to make this call once a year for each patient, so you won't be on the phone for each patient every week.

What Information to Collect or Record While You are On the Phone

Once connected with a representative, you will want to let them know that you are checking on "outpatient mental health benefits". This key phrase will let the representative know to specifically check the patient's plan for nuances regarding mental health benefits.

When completing a verification of benefits it is helpful to have a form to fill out so that you capture all the information that you need to see the patient and be sure that you are going to receive payment from the insurance company. We have included a sample template below to help you in documenting your eligibility and benefits checks. We will go through each section of the E&B template and talk you through what you should document.

Date:
Eligibility and benefit check completed by:

Plan Reset Date and Frequency:

Active insurance: Y/N
Telehealth coverage: Y/N

Authorization Needed
    90791: Y/N
    90837: Y/N
    90834: Y/N
    Additional Codes (if applicable)

Patient Responsibility
    Individual Deductible:
    Family Deductible:
    Copay:

Coinsurance:

Individual Out of Pocket Max:

Family Out of Pocket Max:

Reference number:

Date

You should document the date the E&B check is completed. This will help you know how long it has been since the last check when you or your team members review the information. You will want to compare the date of the last E&B check to the reset date and frequency. The best practice is to complete a full E&B check on the phone once per plan cycle, which in most cases is annually. Once that has been completed, you will want to perform follow-up checks before each session with a patient utilizing an online portal to confirm that the plan is still active, and to update accumulations.

Eligibility and Benefit Check Completed By

This is the name of you or your team member who completed the check. If there is a problem with an E&B check or you need to gain clarification on the information you will know who to go to and ask questions.

Plan Reset Date and Frequency

The date that the insurance plan resets. This can align with a calendar year resetting January 1, or can be any date set by the insurance company. It is typically reset annually, but could have a different renewal frequency.

Active Insurance

You should find out if they have active insurance by providing the representative with the information on the patient's insurance card. If the patient doesn't have active insurance you should stop and ask the patient for updated insurance information. There is no need to find the other information until you have updated insurance information. This will ultimately save you time in the future.

Telehealth Coverage

You will want to note if the patient has telehealth coverage. This is typically a yes or no answer, and will let you know if insurance will reimburse for telehealth sessions or not. The COVID-19 pandemic increased telehealth coverage for many patients, but now it is reverting back and telehealth coverage is not guaranteed. If telehealth sessions are not covered by insurance but you and your patient encounter the need for a telehealth session, knowing whether or not it is covered by insurance can help you and your patient make the best decision for their treatment.

Authorization Needed

You will want to see if any of the codes you bill for need prior authorization. If you see a patient that has insurance that won't pay for a code that requires prior authorization the claim will be denied and you may not receive payment for that service. Be sure to be clear with the system or individual that you are checking benefits with because it is important to get the correct information for this section. 90791, 90837, and 90834 are the most common so we have included them in the template, but depending on the services that you offer you may need to add additional codes to check.

Patient Responsibility

Next you will need to document what the patient will need to pay when they see you for a session, which is called the **Patient Responsibility**. You document the amount the patient should pay in three sections; the **deductible**, the **copay** or **coinsurance** (collectively referred to as **cost sharing**), and the **out of pocket maximum** amount.

Deductibles are the amount that a patient must pay in full before their insurance plan starts covering any costs. For example, if a patient has a $500 deductible, they must pay a sum of $500 for eligible services before their insurance plan starts reimbursing for those services. Services from any type of healthcare provider can apply to the deductible. In rare cases, your patient may have a deductible specifically for Mental Health services, so be on the lookout for this when checking patient benefits. You will want to document the total deductible amount, and the **accumulation**, or how much the patient has contributed to their deductible so far. You will often see this represented as a fraction such as $120/$500, meaning the patient has paid $120 out of their $500 deductible.

Deductible amounts can be for an individual or for a family. If either the individual or family deductible amount has been met, then the patient would owe only a copay or coinsurance. If your patient has not yet met either deductible amount, then they are responsible for paying the entire allowed amount for your session according to your fee schedule. Deductible amounts can vary widely depending on the insurance plan and can reset at the beginning of each plan year. It's important to inform your patients about their deductible and how it may impact their financial responsibility for mental health services.

Cost sharing, or the **copay or coinsurance** is the amount that the patient will pay while the insurance company shares the cost of claims. The copay is a set dollar amount, while the coinsurance is expressed as a percentage of your contracted rate. The insurance company pays the remainder of your allowed amount while the patient is only responsible for the copay or coinsurance amount. Your patient will typically owe a copay OR a coinsurance, not both. Depending on the patient's benefits, they may need to meet their deductible before cost sharing takes place, or the deductible may not apply for mental health benefits and they will skip directly to cost sharing.

The **out-of-pocket maximum** is the full amount the patient needs to pay before the insurance company covers the sessions at 100% leaving the patient to pay 0% of the service. Out-of-pocket maximums are also separated into an individual limit and a family limit. Similar to the deductible, you will want to record both the individual and family out-of-pocket maximums for a patient, and how much they have contributed to each out-of-pocket maximum so far expressed as a fraction. If either the individual or family limit has been met, your patient is fully covered by insurance.

Each level of information is important because it affects what the patient will pay when they see you for services. One of the most important reasons to document this information often is because the contributions that a patient has made to their deductible and out-of-pocket maximums are changing all the time as patients see healthcare providers. It is a good idea to get a clear understanding of how these numbers are changing as the patient sees you over time.

Reference Number and Representative Name

Finally, you will want to ask for and document a reference number for the call from the insurance company and the name of the representative that you spoke to. In the event that you need to circle back with the insurance company for clarity, you can provide the reference number to the new representative so that they can look up their internal records more quickly and directly. You may also want to give that reference to your patient if they want to dispute an eligibility and benefits check. Eligibility and benefit checks provide an estimation of benefits and are not a guarantee of exact payment. The insurance companies reserve the right to change benefits at will, so do not give the patient the expectation that this information is concrete. This information should give the patient a good idea of what they should pay but may not be exactly what they will pay. Your patient is also responsible for knowing their own insurance benefits. We always recommend that patients also check their own benefits.

Want Help with E&B Checks?

Practice Solutions includes Eligibility and Benefit checks with our insurance billing packages. You can hand off the responsibility of calling the insurance company to your biller, and rely on their expertise of asking the right questions to get the most accurate information.

HOW TO INTERPRET ELIGIBILITY AND BENEFIT INFORMATION

Once you have collected the information from the insurance provider, you can practically apply what you learned to calculate what a patient should owe for a session according to their insurance plan. You will collect this amount in the third phase of revenue cycle management, the charge capture phase. In order to calculate this information properly, you will need to know your fee schedule from the insurance company that we discussed in Chapter 3.

Knowing your fee schedule is critical to running a successful practice, especially with the recent implementation of the **No Surprises Act**. Your insurance fee schedule along with eligibility and benefit checks are the greatest tools in providing **good faith estimates** to your patients. Good faith estimates are quotes that you provide to your patient about what they will owe for a session, and they are expected to be provided using the best of your knowledge.

We've mentioned that patient responsibility can be broken down into three phases; the deductible, cost sharing, and full insurance coverage. Your patients may be at different phases within the cycle, and their cycle will reset according to their plan year. We've put together a diagram that you can use to help your patients understand how insurance works and what they are responsible for. You may have some patients who skip the deductible stage if their insurance plan waives the deductible for mental health care.

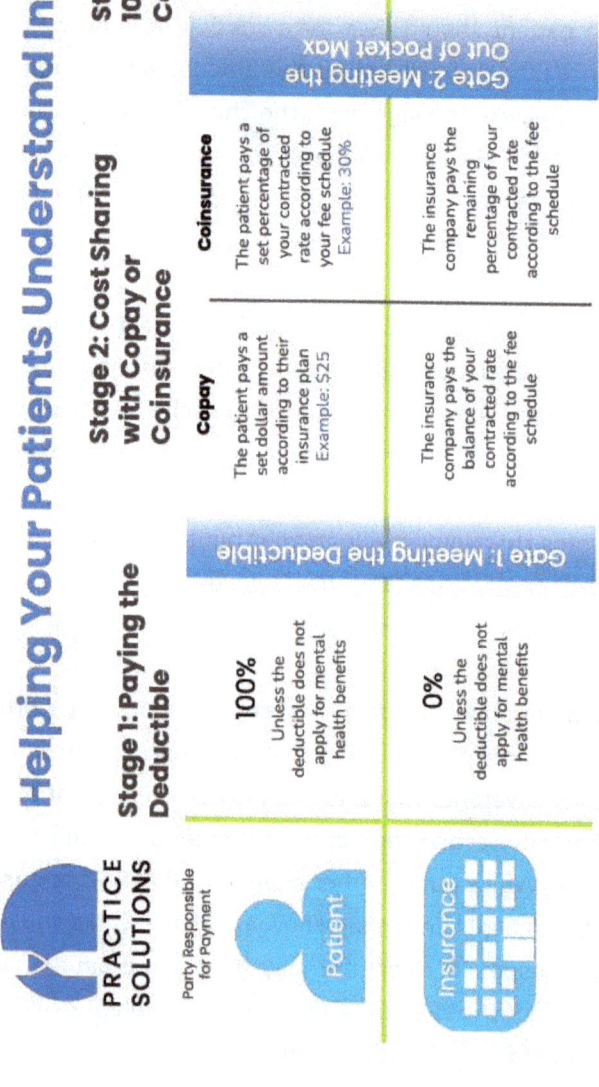

In this section, we will be using hypothetical examples of the Patient Responsibility portion of E&B checks that have been completed for patients, and demonstrating how to use the information to know what the patient owes. In these examples, we are going to assume that you are seeing the patient for a 90791 session, and according to your fee schedule the allowed amount for a 90791 should be $100. We are also assuming that the patient has active insurance coverage.

Your Patient Owes a Deductible

In the first example, you have received the following information regarding the patient's responsibility from the insurance representative.

> Patient Responsibility
> Individual Deductible: $156.34/$500
> Family Deductible: $233.32/$1000
> Copay: $25
> Coinsurance: NA
> Individual Out of Pocket Max: $156.34/$1000
> Family Out of Pocket Max: $233.32/$2000

Your patient has not yet met either their individual or their family deductibles, so they will be responsible for the full cost of the session.

The dollar amount that your patient owes is dictated by the **fee schedule** from the insurance company, otherwise known as the **contracted rate**. Your fee schedule designates that reimbursement for a 90791 is $100. Your patient is responsible for the full $100.

Your patient will be responsible for the full cost of their sessions until the sum of the cost of their medical expenses exceeds their deductible amount, at which point cost sharing will begin.

Your Patient is Cost Sharing With Insurance

If your patient has met either their individual or family deductible, or their plan includes cost sharing for mental health services overpassing their plan deductibles, they will share the cost of their session with their insurance provider. Cost sharing can be done in two methods; your patient will either owe a **copay**, or a **coinsurance**. In either case, the insurance company would pay the remainder of the allowed amount for the session.

Your patient will continue to owe a copay or coinsurance until their costs have met or exceeded their out-of-pocket maximum.

Your Patient Owes a Copay

A **copay** is a set dollar amount designated by the insurance company that your patient would pay every session.

Patient Responsibility

Individual Deductible: $500/$500
Family Deductible: $751/$1000
Copay: $25
Coinsurance: NA
Individual Out of pocket Max: $500/$1000
Family out of pocket Max: $751/$2000

In this example, your patient has met their individual deductible and has a $25 copay. Your patient will owe $25 for the session, and the insurance company will pay the remaining $75 to cover your whole allowed amount of $100.

Your Patient Owes a Coinsurance

A **coinsurance** is a percentage of the allowed amount that your patient would owe. You calculate a coinsurance by consulting your fee schedule for the allowed amount and multiplying the allowed amount by the percentage designated by the insurance company.

Patient Responsibility
Individual Deductible: $260/$500
Family Deductible: $1000/$1000
Copay: NA
Coinsurance: 20%
Individual Out of Pocket Max: $500/$1000
Family Out of Pocket Max: $751/$2000

In this example, your patient has met their $1000 family deductible and owes a 20% coinsurance. To calculate the coinsurance, you take your allowed amount of $100 and multiply it by 0.2 to get $20. Your patient owes $20 for the session, and the insurance company will pay the remaining $80 to cover your whole allowed amount of $100.

Your Patient is Fully Covered by Insurance

Once your patient has met their out of pocket maximum, their sessions will be fully covered by the insurance company. Your patient will no longer owe anything, and the insurance company will pay you the full allowed amount for the session directly.

> Patient Responsibility
> > Individual Deductible: $500/$500
> > Family Deductible:$1000/$1000
> > Copay: NA
> > Coinsurance: ~~20%/~~ Not applicable since OOP has been met
> > Individual Out of pocket Max: $1000/$1000
> > Family out of pocket Max: $1268/$2000

In this example, your patient has met their individual out of pocket maximum, so they are no longer responsible for any portion of payment for services. The insurance company will pay you the entire allowed amount of $100.

CHAPTER SUMMARY

In this chapter you have learned about the idiosyncratic world of eligibility and benefits checks and their importance to your billing process. By ensuring you have the right information and confirming your patients eligibility and benefits you take a big step forward to limiting or eliminating potential billing errors in the process later. You have learned how to understand an eligibility and benefits check and what information needs to be gathered during this process. It is important to remember that eligibility and benefit checks can take time out of your schedule. Therefore, have a plan to outsource that process as soon as it becomes a burden to you.

Follow-Up Actions to Take:

- Collate a list of the best resources for collecting accurate E&B information for each insurance company that you are In-Network with Develop and outline a consistent eligibility and benefits process in your private practice
- Follow through on that process as soon as you have new patients
- Save the eligibility and benefits information in your EHR system
- Review the insurance information with your patients so they have a clear idea of how their insurance is used
- Follow up on any authorization or coordination of benefits requests found in the eligibility and benefit check process

Chapter 7:
COMPLETING SESSIONS

At this point you will have completed the pre-registration phase before the patient comes in your office, collecting patient information, scheduling an appointment, and completing an eligibility and benefit check for the patient. You have completed the registration phase, confirming all information and necessary document collection when the patient arrives at your office. Now comes the part you are familiar with: therapy! You are the expert in this realm; in this section we only aim to help you understand how your therapy sessions fit into the Revenue Cycle Management process, the information that needs to be recorded, and how to record it.

RCM STAGE 3: CHARGE CAPTURE

In Chapter 1, we learned that charge capture refers to collecting payment from your patient. Collecting patient balances is one of the single most important sources of revenue for your practice, and it is one of the most important compliance practices that you can implement. It is important to have a clear and fair billing policy in place for collecting payment from patients. This can help to establish trust and reduce misunderstandings between you and your patients.

When your patient comes in for a session, you will want to use the information you learned in the eligibility and benefit check to collect the appropriate payment from your patient. You can collect this payment before or after the session.

- If your patient has not yet met their deductible and the deductible applies for mental health visits, you should collect the contracted rate according to your fee schedule from the patient.
- If your patient owes a copay, you should collect the copay amount specified by the insurance company.
- If your patient owes a coinsurance amount, you should calculate the percentage of the contracted rate in your fee schedule that the patient owes and charge them that amount.
- If your patient has reached the out of pocket maximum or the services are covered at 100%, they should not owe anything for the session

If you have the eligibility and benefit information prior to your patient arriving, you can collect payment before their session. Many clinicians will opt to have a credit card processor to collect payments, and this function is sometimes built into your EHR. It is also a good idea to have a process in place if the payment method that a patient was using declines. In this case you need to be able to accept cash or a check or another digital form of payment.

If you need to do an E&B check as part of the registration phase when the patient is in your office for a session, an admin could call the insurance company while you are in session and collect from the patient after their session before they leave. If you do not have E&B information yet, you will need to follow up with your patient to collect what they owe for the session. This is why we stress the importance of early eligibility and benefit checks; if you don't collect the correct payment at the time of service, your chance of receiving payment from the patient reduces drastically.

You can consider implementing a policy that allows you to keep a credit card on file for a patient. When you have an exact amount, you can notify the patient and have them authorize the transaction. We would recommend this as a last resort, with the preferred method being to let the patient know what they will owe in advance of the session.

When you collect a payment during charge capture, it is important to record that payment in your EHR, or record it externally to then be recorded in your EHR during the Payment Posting phase. If recording externally, make sure you record the patient name, dollar amount collected, whether the payment was a deductible, copayment or coinsurance, the payment method, and the date of service the payment should apply to. The same information should be recorded in your EHR, but it may be more automated or prompted.

Some patients may not have insurance coverage, or insufficient mental health coverage for their needs. In these cases, and if you are an out-of-network provider to this patient, it is common to collect payment from the patient on a **self-pay** or **private pay** basis, where the patient pays you your cash rate for services. This may involve setting up a payment plan or collecting payment in full at the time of service. You can discuss with your patient whether or not they would like to use their out-of-network benefits and submit a superbill, or if they would prefer to be considered a private pay client and not submit a claim. If you are an in-network provider to that patient, you are contractually obligated to use the patient's insurance.

Some practitioners offer **sliding scale fees**, tailoring their cash rates based on a patient's income and ability to pay. The patient would typically need to complete a "proof of hardship" form to qualify for a sliding scale fee. This can help to make treatment more accessible to those who may otherwise be unable to afford it.

Many therapists have a hard time with this step in the process. We get it! You are in the business of helping people that are having a difficult time, and requiring payment from those people can feel like hurting them. It is important for a wide variety of reasons that you collect payment at this point in the process. First, it is often a contractual obligation with the insurance company if you are In-Network with them. Second, it helps maintain your cash flow which you need to pay your bills. Third, with an effective financial policy your patients should know that services have an associated fee; it is likely that they expected to pay for treatment even before seeking care. Finally, collecting payment up front makes sure the patient understands the worth of your time and the services you provide. Your work is valuable, and you should not feel compelled to work for free.

It is important to clearly communicate your billing policy to patients before beginning treatment. This can help to avoid misunderstandings and ensure that patients are aware of their financial responsibilities. Overall, the goal should be to collect payment in a way that is fair and respectful to both you and your patients.

CODING FOR BILLING

For any therapy sessions, you will need to know the codes the insurance company uses to identify services. These codes will need to be entered into your EHR, documented for each session, and verified and updated at the end of the session. In this section, we will be discussing common codes and billing practices used in the field of mental health. It is important for mental health professionals to have a solid understanding of these codes and practices, as they play a vital role in the delivery of mental health services and the reimbursement of those services. By the end of this chapter, you should have a good understanding of the different codes used in mental health billing, as well as the importance of accurate and ethical coding practices.

How to Code

Coding refers to the translation of the service that you provided for a patient to a billing code, also called a **Current Procedural Terminology (CPT) Code.** These codes are standardized and designated by the **American Medical Association (AMA)** and used to communicate medical, surgical, and diagnostic services provided to patients to insurance companies.

As a mental health provider, it is your responsibility to accurately document the services you provide to your patients in your EHR utilizing these CPT Codes. Coding for sessions in your EHR is vital to billing and reimbursement for your practice. It also allows you to track trends and patterns in mental health treatment such as the types of services you offer, the duration of each session, and the frequency of sessions.

There are several steps to coding for sessions in your EHR:

1. Identify the appropriate code(s) for the corresponding therapy session.
2. Enter the code(s) for the session into your EHR. This process may vary depending on the EHR you are using, but most EHRs have a designated field for entering codes. Simply type in the appropriate code for the service provided.
3. Document the length of a session in the appropriate data field in your EHR.
4. Record codes for additional services such as medication management.

5. Add any necessary modifiers to codes.
6. Save and submit, and verify that the information has been recorded.

Modifiers are extensions to CPT codes that communicate additional information about a session to an insurance company. A common modifier is one indicating a telehealth session, and can either be represented as 95 or GT, depending on the insurance company's specifications. Another common modifier is HJ, indicating an EAP session. There are also some modifiers that indicate a provider's license type. Always check with your contract to see what modifiers might apply to the services you provide.

You will need to choose the appropriate code for the corresponding therapy session. Most EHRs have a designated field for entering codes. Simply type in the appropriate code for the service provided. If you provided additional services during the session, such as a medication management review, be sure to document these as well. Once you have entered all the necessary information, be sure to save and submit the documentation to ensure it is properly recorded in your EHR.

By following these steps, you can accurately and efficiently code for sessions in your EHR. This will not only help with tracking and billing for your practice, but also provide a clear record of the services you have provided to your patients.

Common CPT Codes Used in Mental Health

It is important to have a thorough understanding of common **Current Procedural Terminology (CPT) codes** used in your field. There are a variety of codes available for different types of mental health services. Until you are familiar with the codes that you use, it can be helpful to keep a reference sheet. Some common codes include:

- 90791: Psychiatric Diagnostic Evaluation, 60 minutes
- 90832: Psychotherapy, 30 minutes with patient and/or family member
- 90834: Psychotherapy, 45 minutes with patient and/or family member
- 90837: Psychotherapy, 60 minutes with patient and/or family member
- 90846: Family psychotherapy (conjoint psychotherapy) (with the patient present)
- 90847: Family psychotherapy (without the patient present)
- 90853: Group psychotherapy
- 90875: Interactive complexity
- 90876: Interactive complexity, requiring additional time with the patient and/or family member
- 90887: Coordination of care with multiple healthcare providers (e.g., consultation with other mental health professionals)

In this section, we will define some of the most commonly used CPT codes in mental health, including those for individual, group and family therapy sessions, as well as codes for assessments and evaluations. This is by no means an exhaustive list, and it is the responsibility of the mental health provider to stay up-to-date on all relevant CPT codes for their practice.

Individual Therapy CPT Codes

90834: This code is used for individual psychotherapy sessions lasting 45-50 minutes. It is the most commonly used code for individual therapy sessions and can be used for a wide range of mental health conditions.

90837: This code is used for individual psychotherapy sessions lasting 60 minutes. It is typically used when longer sessions are required due to the complexity of the patient's treatment plan.

90847: This code is used for family therapy sessions with the patient present, lasting 45-50 minutes. It is often used when family dynamics are a significant factor in the patient's mental health treatment.

Group Therapy CPT Codes

90853: This code is used for group psychotherapy sessions lasting 60 minutes. It is commonly used for group therapy formats such as cognitive-behavioral therapy (CBT) or dialectical behavior therapy (DBT).

Assessments and Evaluations CPT Codes

90791: This code is an intake code used for psychiatric diagnostic evaluations, including interviews and assessments of the patient's mental health history and current symptoms. When entering a therapeutic relationship, you will likely use this code for your initial session.

90792: This code is used for psychiatric diagnostic evaluations with medical services, such as a physical examination or lab tests.

Psychological Testing

96136: First 30 minutes of admin and scoring for a psychological test.
+96137: Each additional 30 minutes of admin and scoring for a psychological test.

96130: First hour of evaluation and feedback for a psychological test.
+96131: Each additional hour of psychological testing.

Neuropsychological Testing

96136: First 30 minutes of admin and scoring for a psychological test.
+96137: Each additional 30 minutes of admin and scoring for a psychological test.

96132: First hour of evaluation and feedback for a psychological test.

+96132: Each additional hour of psychological testing.

These codes may have specific documentation requirements and may be subject to medical necessity review by insurance companies. It is your responsibility to accurately and thoroughly document the services provided to your patients in order to ensure proper reimbursement and compliance with insurance guidelines.

COMPLETING NOTES

Once a session is complete, you will want to complete a **progress note**. A progress note in a mental health practice is a concise, structured record that documents a patient's session content, therapeutic interventions, and the patient's progress toward treatment goals. It serves as a vital tool for therapists to track the course of therapy, assess the effectiveness of interventions, and ensure continuity of care. Progress notes typically include a diagnosis (Dx code) and procedure code (CPT Code), the date of the session along with start time and end time, a summary of the session content, any assessments or observations made by the therapist, the patient's response to treatment, and the therapist's plan for future sessions. These notes are essential for maintaining accurate and thorough patient records, facilitating collaboration among treatment providers, and meeting ethical and legal standards of care.

You can complete your notes in whatever format works best for you, whether that be in your EHR or on paper, but a progress note must be completed and have a CPT and Dx code before a claim can be billed. If you completed your note outside of your EHR, you will need to indicate "note completed externally." Keeping up with progress notes is often one of the biggest barriers for providers when it comes to submitting claims within the timely filing limits established by the insurance company. We've compiled some suggestions to help you stay on top of your notes based on the experience we have working with our billing clients.

You may find it helpful to schedule blocks of time in your workweek to complete notes. Treat this as a commitment on the same level as an appointment with a patient, and do not double book in the time you have allotted to complete your notes. You may find that it's easier to block out short amounts of time after each session, or that you want to block out a larger amount of time each day to work on your notes. You will learn what works best for you and how much time you need to dedicate to your notes as you complete more sessions.

When it comes to notes, there are two ways that you can think about it: as a long list of notes that need to go out, OR as a long list of paychecks that could be coming in! Sometimes rather than looking at the task at hand, it can be helpful to look at the monetary reward as a motivator. One note done = $80 in the bank!

When you've got notes to do, always complete the oldest note that you have to do first, and work your way to the more recent notes. This can prevent older notes slipping through the cracks and potentially missing timely filing limits. As a therapist, there is an ethical responsibility to complete notes in a timely manner.

Some group practices have employment contracts that indicate deadlines for note completion and consequences for missing those deadlines, such as a reduction in compensation for every day that a note is late. This can be an effective incentive for getting your providers to complete their notes on time.

Goal setting can also be a powerful tool to incentivize! We have seen providers in Group Practices use goals around completing notes as friendly competition- the result is that no one ends up behind! Example goals can be "Write 5 Notes per day" or "Keep the average time for note completion less than 24 hours from the time of the session." Writing these goals down and sharing these goals with another person can help you to stay on track. Try to push yourself when goal-setting and go a little bit outside of your comfort zone. Make sure this goal is something that you can easily measure, and check in against your goal often. The more disciplined you are about checking in with your goals, the more likely you are to build good habits around note writing.

CHAPTER SUMMARY

In this chapter you have learned about coding for your sessions according to industry best-practices. You have learned about what is necessary to complete your sessions and how you ought to complete your notes. This is a critical part of the billing process because many EHR systems will not let you create or submit a claim without the completion of a session note. Here are our best recommendations for completing notes.

Follow-Up Actions to Take

- Set aside time every day to complete your notes
- Ensure accuracy in your coding by double checking your work
- Ensure the code you are using aligns with the service you performed

Chapter 8:
RCM STAGE 4: CLAIM SUBMISSION

Once you have completed a session, coded the session for billing, and completed a progress note, you are ready to submit a claim to the insurance company! Claim submission, as we learned in chapter 1, is the process by which all information about your session with a patient is transmitted to the insurance company so that the insurance company can review and remit any necessary payment.

In this chapter, we will define both a paper and electronic claim, identify all of the information that needs to be included on a claim and discuss the submission methods for paper and electronic claims. We will also talk about where a claim goes once it is submitted and some troubleshooting tips to keep in mind as you are submitting claims.

WHAT IS A CLAIM?

A **claim** serves to provide information about a patient's healthcare services to their insurance company, allowing the insurance company to track and fulfill the benefits guaranteed by a patient's insurance plan. A claim is submitted as a standardized form filled out to an insurance company and can serve to notify the insurance company of any payment owed to a healthcare provider or patient.

In the United States Healthcare system there are actually two types of claim forms. There is a CMS 1500 form and a UB-04 form. The claim form system was developed to help identify the procedures being performed on patients and who was performing them, however, there is a difference between hospital services and professional outpatient services. This is why there are two kinds of claim forms. As an outpatient mental health provider, you will largely be dealing with CMS 1500 forms, or their electronic counterpart the ANSI-X12-837.

WHAT INFORMATION IS ON A CLAIM?

There are three categories of information that need to be included on a claim form: patient information, session information, and provider/practice information. You will recognize that a lot of the information needed for a claim form has been discussed in previous chapters; the billing process is designed to collect and record all of the necessary information so that claim forms can be filled out and submitted efficiently.

Patient Information

Insurance Type (Medicare, Medicaid, or Private Insurance)
Insurance ID Number

Patient Name as shown on the insurance card (Last Name, First Name, Middle Initial)
Patient Birthdate
Patient Sex
Name of Subscriber
Patient's Address
Patient's Relationship to the Subscriber
Address of the Subscriber/Policyholder
Secondary Insurance Information (If applicable)
Insurance Group Number
Birthdate of the Subscriber
Amount Paid (Either deductible, copay, or coinsurance amount charged to the patient)

Session Information

Diagnosis Code(s)
Is this a resubmission of a claim?
Did the service require authorization?
Date of Service
Place of Service
CPT Codes for the type of session
Any necessary Modifiers
The Amount you Charged

Provider Information

NPI Number (Individual and/or Group)

Tax ID (Either SSN or EIN, depending on how you are credentialed)
Office Name
Office Address
Your Name
Medicare PTAN (If applicable)
Medicaid Provider ID (If applicable)

Each piece of information will need to be recorded on the corresponding box of the CMS 1500 form or entered into your EHR to generate an electronic claim. There are a few things that you should consider when you are reviewing the information for a claim.

Name

Does your name have an uncommon spelling, or include a middle initial? Have you legally changed your name recently? Has your business changed its name, or does it operate under an acronym? These are all possible circumstances that could yield issues in the "key" not matching the "lock" when it comes to insurance claim processing. Double check that when you are credentialing, the information that you include in your name for either yourself or your business is recorded correctly so that you can include the exact same information on every claim submitted.

National Provider Identifier

The NPI, otherwise known as the National Provider identifier, is a ten digit number that every therapist filing insurance claims should have. This number is not specific to therapists; every healthcare provider who is submitting insurance claims should have an NPI number. In the past, providers had different identification numbers for each insurance company. In order to standardize, the National Plan and Provider Enumeration system was developed to assign providers one identifier that they would use across all insurance companies. That being said, there are two different types of NPI number and a provider may have both types. If you are unsure of your NPI number, or which type of NPI number it is, you can reference the NPPES NPI Registry to look up your information.

NPI Type 1
This is otherwise known as an Individual NPI. Every provider who intends to credential with an insurance company and submit claims for reimbursement should have a type 1 NPI, even if they are part of a group.

NPI Type 2
This is otherwise known as the Group NPI. This NPI gets assigned to a group organization so that many providers can submit under a single NPI. Not every provider will have a group NPI. If your practice chooses to bill as a group, the individual NPI may still appear on the claim as

the rendering provider, but the group NPI would be used as the billing NPI.

Tax ID Number

The tax ID number is a government issued ID number used for tax purposes. Checks issued from the insurance company are like paychecks, and the Tax ID must be associated with these payments to report income. There are two different types of Tax ID that you may have, but you must have one or the other registered with an insurance company.

Social Security Number (SSN)
The Social Security Number is your own personal social security number issued by the IRS, formatted XXX-XX-XXXX. In general we do not recommend using your SSN as your tax ID as this number will show up on any superbills that a patient can see and can open you up to risk of identity theft. Instead, we recommend that you apply for an EIN as a solo practitioner. If you are already credentialed using your SSN you can submit claims using your SSN, but you may still want to consider applying for an EIN and updating this with the insurance company.

Employer Identification Number (EIN)
The EIN is also a nine digit number, formatted XX-XXXXXXX issued by the IRS. In order to obtain an EIN number, you must fill out an application with the IRS using your business information. Even if you are a solo practitioner,

you can still apply for an EIN rather than using your SSN for credentialing and billing. Once you complete the application and it is reviewed, the IRS will issue your EIN number, which should be kept with the same regard as your SSN. Keep this number protected, but also have it readily available for billing purposes!

Address

Your address is one of the identifiers for your "key" to billing, yet is often the most problematic because it can be difficult to remember to update it when you move, or start operating out of an office instead of your home. When you credential, make note of the address that was used. If your practice ever starts operating from a different address, make sure to update your credentials to reflect the new address and update your practice location on the claim form or in your EHR so that claims get sent with your new address.

Billing Address

The billing address is typically the address where you or your office are physically located, and is used for claim submission. Unless you have a separate mailing address on file, this is where all important information will be sent to you by the insurance company, including paper checks if that is your preferred reimbursement method.

Mailing Address

Insurance companies may allow you to have a separate mailing address established. This can be helpful if you would prefer to have all correspondence sent to a specific address such as a home address, but have been credentialed using a different address such as an office address. As long as you are still associated with both locations, you can establish a mailing address, yet still use the billing address on the claim submission form so that the claim can be properly processed.

If you ever decide to move, either your billing address or your mailing address, and you are no longer associated with a specific address, always be sure to update this information with the insurance company as soon as possible in order to avoid any confusion.

Insurance Specific Identifiers

Medicare: PTAN

If you applied to be a Medicare Administrative Contractor and your application was approved, you will have been issued a Provider Transaction Access Number (PTAN). This number will need to be included on claim submissions to Medicare.

Medicaid: Provider ID
In some states, the Medicaid Provider ID is just the NPI number that you used to credential with. In other states, Medicaid will issue a separate Provider ID number that will need to be included on claim submissions.

Other Insurance Providers
It is not very common, but there are a few other insurance companies that will issue you their own identifying numbers. When you are credentialed and you receive any contracts, welcome packets, or correspondence indicating that you are credentialed, read everything carefully and keep an eye out for identifying numbers that may be important to store.

Taxonomy Codes

If you are a Medicare provider, you will need to know your taxonomy code. This is something that you will need to know in order to apply to be a medicare provider, and the taxonomy code submitted on any claims must match the taxonomy code that was submitted on your application to become a Medicare provider. Your taxonomy code is determined by the type of provider you are, as well as your specialty. If you do not already know your taxonomy code, you can review this article (https://www.cms.gov/medicare/enrollment-renewal/providers-suppliers/health-care-taxonomy) from the Centers for Medicare and Medicaid Services website.

HOW TO SUBMIT A CLAIM

There are two ways that claims can be submitted; by paper, or electronically. In today's digital world, the electronic claim is the preferable method of claim submission with several advantages over paper claims. In this section we will discuss both methods of claim submission and the pros and cons of both.

Once you know that your patient is eligible for reimbursement for services, your notes and documentation is completed, and a clean claim has been created, then feel free to submit the claim to insurance and wait for a response from the insurance company. There is a lot of administrative work that is invested in ensuring claims process for payment, but we are confident that it can be done.

Actually submitting claims to the insurance company is functionally easy, but did you know that sometimes a patient's eligibility can change? This means that while you think you are going to submit a clean claim you could not be. This is why we recommend that you check the patient's eligibility and benefits before submitting a claim.

Paper Claim

For the longest time paper claims were the dominant method of being reimbursed. To this day some mental health providers still utilize paper claims, but that number is dwindling. Many insurance companies are beginning to adopt policies that restrict the use of paper claims.

Outside of payer policies, paper claims have become expensive and require significantly more cost to the practice owner than electronic claims. Between the cost of the claim form, an envelope and postage, an individual paper claim could cost up to $1.04, and about 10 minutes of your time to fill out and mail. Alternatively, electronic claim submission has a nominal charge (often less than $0.25) and takes significantly less time.

There are a few instances in which paper claims are necessary, such as your EHR not being compatible with digital submission for an insurance company or in the event of a secondary insurance requiring a paper claim, among others. In those cases you will want to generate a CMS 1500 form from your EHR filled in with all of the required information. It is a standardized red form with boxes where each piece of information can be reported. You can print the document generated by your EHR onto an official blank claim form, which can be found at https://www.cms.gov/medicare/billing/electronicbillingeditrans/1500.

Once the form is filled out completely and accurately, you will want to place it in an envelope with appropriate postage. The envelope should be addressed to the designated claims address, which can either be found on the back of your patient's insurance card or in your contract from the insurance company. If you are in doubt of which address a paper claim form should be sent to, you can verify by calling the insurance company.

Before submitting a paper claim, check and see if there are other viable options for submission. Sometimes you are able to fax a CMS form to the insurance company or submit through an insurance company portal, which will be faster than mailing.

Electronic Claim

An electronic claim is the preferred method for most insurance companies and providers. Electronic claims provide an added level of security in data transmission, they are cost effective, and they can drastically shorten the time to payment as long as all information submitted on the claim is correct.

To submit an electronic claim, you will need to use your EHR to generate an electronic claim file, which is known as an ANSI-X12-837. You can either export and submit this file through an insurance portal, or you can submit the claim directly through your EHR if you have your EDI connection set up as instructed in Chapter 4.

I know what you are thinking, "Isn't it as easy as pressing a button?"

Unfortunately, no, it is not as easy as pressing a button. **Claim scrubbing**, or double checking the claim information before sending, is one of the best ways to prevent errors. You will want to verify the claim information against an eligibility and benefit check and against the copy of the patient's insurance card. The ultimate goal is to submit a **clean claim**, which is a claim without any errors that can be processed and paid immediately by the insurance company.

Your patient's situation can change in a matter of days; they could meet a deductible, they could change jobs or any number of reasons could change their insurance coverage between the completion of the E&B check and claim submission. There are a few best practices you can implement to make sure you are **scrubbing** your claims before sending them.

Additionally, don't assume that you or your staff executed the process perfectly. What if you or your clinician accidentally miscoded a claim and now you have to correct that down the road? What if the rate on the claim was the incorrect amount?

There are a lot of things that can go wrong with the insurance claim submission process, and making sure that you have a quality control procedure in place will ensure that you are paid in a timely manner and don't have to fix mistakes later.

Superbills

A superbill can be generated if a patient needs to submit their own claim to the insurance company. You would need to provide the necessary information on a superbill for the patient to then submit. This is typically used for out-of-network patients.

Remember Your Timely Filing Limits

In Chapter 3, we discussed that you should make note of your timely filing limits. It is in the claim submission stage that these timely filing limits become very important. You need to make sure that you are submitting your claims according to the deadlines set by each of your insurance companies.

For example, let's say you have a patient that has BCBS and you are in-network with BCBS. BCBS has a 180 day timely filing limit. That means that you have 180 days to submit the claims for your patient to BCBS and are eligible for processing.

So, if you have a session with your patient today and you submit the claim today then you would be within the timely filing limits, but if you were to see the patient today and submit the claim 181 days from now the insurance company would deny the claim for being outside the timely filing limits. Many insurance companies have timely filing limits that are much shorter, even as short as 30 days.

We do not suggest waiting the full length of timely filing to submit your claims. It is best for the cash flow of your practice to submit claims on a regular schedule relatively soon after your session. Practice Solutions operates on a biweekly billing schedule, submitting claims every two weeks in batches. **Batching claims** means that information for multiple sessions or patients with the same insurance are sent on the same electronic claim. This can provide small cost savings to providers, as there is typically a nominal fee for each electronic claim submitted in your EHR.

If the insurance company gave you a year to submit claims for services rendered but you did not get around to it, the insurance company shouldn't be on the hook for those claims indefinitely. They have to set parameters around what they are responsible for and what they are not responsible for. Missing timely filing deadlines is lost revenue for your practice. The strategies outlined in this book are designed to help you avoid issues with timely filing.

Knowing the timely filing limits helps you to keep your revenue stable throughout your time in taking insurance and lowers the amounts of denials that you receive from the insurance company. Even if you or your biller receive a timely filing denial there is no chance of appealing that claim and receiving payment.

THE ROLE OF A CLEARINGHOUSE IN CLAIM SUBMISSION

A clearinghouse is a third-party organization that scrubs, reformats and transmits claims as a middle man between the EHR and the payer. The role of a clearinghouse in claim submission is to ensure that the claims are complete, accurate, and formatted properly for the payer, whether it be a private insurance company or a government healthcare program such as Medicare or Medicaid. Clearinghouses are largely only involved in electronic claims, with very few being involved in paper claims.

Before an electronic claim is submitted to the payer, it must first go through a third-party clearinghouse. This clearinghouse is responsible for reviewing the claim to make sure it is complete and accurate, and for formatting the claim in a way that is compatible with the payer's system. The clearinghouse may also perform various checks on the claim, such as verifying the patient's insurance coverage and ensuring that the charges are within the allowed amounts for the services provided.

Once the claim has been reviewed and processed by the clearinghouse, it is then transmitted to the payer's internal clearinghouse for review and payment. The third-party clearinghouse may also track the status of the claim and follow up with the payer if there are any issues or delays in payment.

Clearinghouses can speed up the payment process by ensuring that claims are complete and accurate when they are submitted, reducing the number of denied or rejected claims that require follow-up. Clearinghouses provide standardization to the claims submission process, ensuring that claim data is formatted and transmitted in a way that is compatible with the payer's system, further speeding up the claim process. Overall, clearinghouses remove some of the administrative burden from providers by supplying another layer of claim scrubbing to catch as many errors as possible before the claim reaches the insurance company.

There are many different clearinghouses available, and healthcare providers can choose the one that best meets their needs. Some clearinghouses may specialize in certain types of claims or payers, while others may offer a more comprehensive range of services. It is important for healthcare providers to carefully research and select a clearinghouse that is reputable and reliable. You may also want to consider which clearinghouses are compatible with your EHR. If you choose a clearinghouse that is not compatible with your EHR, you will not be able to utilize EDI transactions to submit claims electronically, which can add time and room for error in the billing process. You also may incur additional costs if you choose to use a clearinghouse that is not affiliated with your EHR.

In summary, the role of a clearinghouse in claim submission is to review, format, and transmit claims on behalf of healthcare providers. Using a clearinghouse can help to speed up the payment process, reduce the risk of errors or delays, and reduce the administrative burden on healthcare providers. It is important for providers to carefully research and select a clearinghouse that meets their needs and is reliable.

CHAPTER SUMMARY

In this chapter you have learned about the claim submission process. This process becomes much easier with the right organization and proper preparation for clean claim submission. You have learned what a claim is, what information is needed for a claim to be submitted, and you have learned the technological process for how a claim is sent and processed by an insurance company. Here are some actionable suggestions we have for you to maintain a healthy claim submission process.

Follow-Up Actions to Take:

- Prior to submitting a claim, double check the patient's information
- Double check the codes used and verify their accuracy
- Double check your information to ensure it is accurate to your credentialing information

Chapter 9:
RCM STAGE 5: PAYMENT POSTING

The next three stages of revenue cycle management are dependent on what path the claim takes once it has been submitted to the insurance company. If the claim is processed and paid, you would then move on to payment posting, where you record in your EHR how the insurance company processed the claim and what was paid.

EOB OR ERA

When an insurance company processes a claim, they will communicate how it has been processed in either a paper **Explanation of Benefits (EOB)** or an **Electronic Remittance Advice (ERA)**. These are two terms for the same type of information, delivered in different formats. It will inform you if the claim has been accepted or denied and outline the costs of the treatment, any insurance coverage that was applied and any amount that the patient is responsible for paying.

Explanation of Benefits (EOB)

An EOB is a paper form that provides a summary of how a claim or claims have been processed and paid by an insurance company. Paper EOBs deliver the same information as their electronic counterparts, but are more time consuming to receive through the mail and process into your EHR. For this reason, we encourage you to enroll to receive ERAs in your EHR for as many payers as you are able to.

Electronic Remittance Advice (ERA)

The ERA is the most efficient way to receive information on processed claims, as it gets delivered directly to your EHR and information can be matched and posted quickly and accurately. Electronic communication between an insurance company and your EHR is all encrypted and HIPAA compliant.

In chapter 4, you learned that ERA enrollment is something that you can set up in preparation for billing. It is best to enroll before you start billing, but you can enroll to receive ERAs at any time with your In Network payers. Some insurance companies will not finalize ERA enrollment until you are ready to submit a claim. In this case, you can finish the paperwork and finalize the enrollment after your first session with a patient with this insurance. If you make any changes to how you are credentialed and billing, such as switching from an individual NPI to a group NPI, you will need to re-enroll with the new information to continue to receive ERA. If you have providers billing under individual NPI and tax ID information, an ERA enrollment form will need to be completed for each provider. Lastly, if you credential with any new insurance payers throughout your career you will need to complete new enrollments.

Practice Solutions not only helps our clients with the initial ERA setup, but manages any additional ERA enrollments needed and resolves any unexplained disruptions to ERA service.

HOW TO READ AND INTERPRET EOBS AND ERAS

Once you receive your EOB or ERA, take the time to carefully review it. Make sure that all of the information is accurate and that all of the charges listed are for services that you actually rendered. If you notice any errors or discrepancies, contact the insurance company to have them corrected. Before you can accurately post the EOB or ERA, it is important to understand the details of the patient's insurance coverage. This includes the deductible, co-payments, and co-insurance. When you run an eligibility & benefit check, the insurance company will provide you with a summary of the coverage for any services you request and will indicate to you if there are any limitations or exclusions.

The EOB or ERA should clearly state the amount that the insurance company will cover and the amount that the patient is responsible for paying. If they have met their deductible for the year, the insurance company will likely cover a larger portion of the costs. If the patient has not met their deductible, they will be responsible for paying the full cost of services until the deductible is met.

There are several components that you will want to look for on an EOB or ERA. These will be reported differently based on which document you are referencing, and which insurance company it came from. EOBs or ERAs may also have other categories of information outside of the ones listed here, and you should familiarize yourself with all components so that you can fully understand what is being communicated.

Dates of Service

An EOB or ERA can contain information from multiple dates of service.

Procedure Code

This will indicate which procedure code(s) are being paid or not paid.

Charged Amount

This amount is what was billed to the insurance company. It should reflect your standard cash rate.

Allowed Amount

The **allowed amount** is the amount that the insurance company is indicating is allowed as payment for this service. This should match the contracted rate on your fee schedule. If it does not, the insurance company may have processed the claim incorrectly or you need to obtain an updated copy of your fee schedule. It is extremely helpful for you to have a copy of your fee schedule so that you can verify that you are getting paid what you should be getting paid by the insurance company according to your contract.

Patient Responsibility or Subscriber Amount

This is the amount that your patient should pay or should have already paid toward the session. This amount should match the information you received in the E&B check.

Amount Paid

This is the amount that was paid for the session by the insurance company. Amount paid and patient responsibility should add up to the allowed amount.

Adjusted Amount

The **Adjusted Amount** is the difference between the submitted rate and the allowed amount. For example, if you would charge a private pay client $150.00 for a 90837 session but the insurance company only allows $100.00 there will be a $50.00 "adjusted amount". That adjusted amount is the cost of doing business with insurance on an in-network basis.

PAYMENT POSTING

Payment Posting refers to recording the payment information from the EOB or ERA or any external patient payments into your EHR for corresponding sessions. It is important to record payments or non-payments so that you can have an accurate understanding of revenue for your practice. In this stage, you may also discover denials and will want to record them for the next phase, claim follow-up.

Posting Insurance Payments

For any ERA or EOB you receive, you will need to evaluate whether to post a payment and close out the date of service, or to record a denial and investigate the date of service further.

For any date of service that has an allowed amount that matches your contracted rate on the fee schedule, you should record the insurance amount in your EHR. This will include the amount paid and any adjustment amount. If the allowed amount is listed and matches your contracted rate but the insurance amount is zero, then the claim did process and is not a denied claim. A zero dollar insurance payment should be recorded, and the patient should be indicated to owe the full amount which would be applied to their deductible.

When the Amount Paid is zero dollars and there is no allowed amount listed, this would indicate a denied claim. Do not post this payment, but externally record the denial for future follow-up.

Posting Patient Payments

If the EOB or ERA indicates that the patient owes an amount, first check to make sure that the patient amount on the EOB or ERA matches what the E&B check indicated. If the amounts don't match, you will need to check the insurance company portal to reconfirm the patient's payment responsibility and/or contact the insurance company to clarify which amount is correct. If the amounts match, you should then check whether or not a payment has been collected from your patient in the charge capture phase.

If they have submitted a payment that has been recorded in your EHR, verify that the amount matches what was on the EOB or ERA. If these amounts truly don't match, your patient will either owe a balance (they underpaid) or they will have a credit to their account (they overpaid). You will want to contact them immediately to rectify the balance. If the amounts do match, then no further action is necessary.

If a patient payment is not recorded in your EHR and you have a process to record patient payments externally, look for a record of payment there. If you find a match, enter the amount into your EHR. Again, you will want to make sure that the paid amount matches what was indicated as patient responsibility on the EOB or ERA.

If the patient has not made the payment indicated on the EOB or ERA, they will need to make a payment. If you have a credit card on file, you can charge the card according to your financial policy. Otherwise, you will need to follow up with the patient according to Stage 7: Outstanding Patient Collections covered in Chapter 11.

You should keep a copy of your EOB or ERA for your records. This will allow you to track your healthcare payments and make sure that you are collecting accurately. It can also be useful if you need to file an appeal or dispute a charge with the insurance company.

RECEIVING PAYMENTS

The EOB or ERA will tell you what payment you will receive, but funds may be received separately from the EOB or ERA as it is only a detailed record of the payment being issued. How you get paid is typically established during the credentialing process. You can always make updates to your payment method by reaching out to the Provider Services Department of the insurance company. Each insurance company does things differently, so be sure to clarify all steps of the process with the representative to get your payment preferences updated accurately.

Paper Checks

Many insurance companies will issue paper checks that get mailed directly to the billing address of your organization. The paper checks will typically come with a paper EOB. Checks can then be deposited by traditional bank deposit methods.

Many people like the traditional paper check because they feel it gives them a more hands-on approach to their money, but there are some disadvantages to paper checks.

In order to reliably receive paper checks, your billing address must be accurate with the insurance company. If your company has moved, or is planning on moving, there can be some unreliability in getting the address updated in time before checks are issued.

Additionally, if you were previously credentialed under a group practice but have transitioned to working in your own private practice, there is a chance that paper checks could be mailed to your previous group practice if you were credentialed using that group practice's address.

The last pitfall is the reliance on the U.S. Postal System. We've all got a story of something that's been delayed or lost in the mail. If funds are needed in a timely manner, you may be better off using electronic payment methods.

Electronic Funds Transfer (EFT)

There has been a rise in the availability of EFT payments from insurance companies. An **EFT**, or **Electronic Funds Transfer**, is a direct deposit into your bank account from the insurance company. This method typically tends to process faster, and there are added security measures with electronic payments. Different insurance companies use different methods of setting up the EFT payments, but these are frequently set up through online portals that require an account with a username and password. Typically you will need a voided check with routing number and account number for the bank account that you would like payments directed to in order to get this set up. Again, reaching out to the Provider Services Department of the insurance company and asking how you enroll in EFT is the best way to make sure that all steps of the process are completed properly.

Sometimes enrolling in EFT is required in order to receive ERA, and both enrollments can be completed at the same time. We always recommend that providers complete this enrollment when available, as digital methods for receiving payment and ERA are much faster.

Although you don't have to worry about the reliability of the postal system or having your check delivered to an incorrect address, you do need to make sure that your banking information is up to date with the insurance company. If you ever have any changes to your bank account, or you decide to start using a new financial institution, remember to update the insurance company to keep receiving payments properly.

Getting the EFT payments set up can sometimes be a bit more complicated, and can involve working with the insurance company as well as your bank to get things functioning properly. Since each insurance company has a slightly different enrollment process, it can feel tedious to get set up.

Virtual Cards

Virtual cards are the least common type of payment, and are usually the least preferred. These payments are sent in a format similar to a credit card, with an account number and security code. It can come in a digital or paper format, and will include an image of a card. The intent with these payments is that you would charge the "card" in your credit card processing system as if it were a credit card payment using the information provided to you.

These types of payments are processed through a third party program, the most common one being Zelis.

As mentioned above, these payments are usually not preferred for several reasons. Firstly, it is assumed that you have a credit card processing system to run the information through. There are typically fees to process card payments which apply to the virtual card payments as well. This means that you would not be receiving your full contracted rate after processing the card and paying the credit card fees.

The last challenge with the virtual card payment system is that it can make record keeping difficult. The insurance company needs to be added as a "client" in your system in order to process the payment. It can then be difficult to match the payment back to the corresponding session to reflect a paid status. Any amounts posted would also need to be reconciled for credit card processing fees.

AGING REPORTS

Aging reports show you any sessions that have unpaid balances and how old those balances are. Payment posting in a detailed and timely manner helps you to have accurate aging reports, giving you a better chance to identify and resolve problems with specific insurance companies or patients. There are two types of aging reports: the insurance aging report and the patient aging report.

Insurance Aging Report

Your **Insurance Aging Report** is a report of insurance sessions that have not yet had payments posted and are considered "open". The way that the Aging Report is generated can vary depending on the EHR, but typically a session will be reflected on your aging report as of the date of service, and will remain on the aging report until payment has been received and posted for a submitted claim. It is a tool that you can use to understand how many insurance payments are outstanding.

The Aging Report is organized in rows for each insurance company, and columns of the "age" of outstanding amounts. These ages are 0-15 Days, 15-30 Days, 31-60 Days, 61-90 Days, 91-120 Days, and 120+ Days. Total outstanding amounts will be reflected by insurance company and age.

Insurance Company	0-15 Days	15-30 Days	31-60 Days	61-90 Days	91-120 Days	120+ Days	Total
Insurance A	$1000	$800	$500	$300	$100	$0	$2700
Insurance B	$500	$350	$200	$400	$0	$600	$2050

Keep in mind that the aging reports typically show the full cash value of a session rather than the expected contracted amount from insurance. This is why fee schedules are a more valuable tool in revenue projections, since the Aging Report can show an inflated number that does not actually reflect what you will receive in payment. In other words, the aging report does not account for any adjusted amounts to your standard cash rate.

When you are not posting payments, your aging report is meaningless. In order for it to be useful, you need to post payments regularly so that the aging report detail only includes claims that truly have not yet been paid, and follow-up activity can be focused.

If all the steps in the revenue cycle management process are not successfully completed, or if they are completed poorly, then you might see a high dollar value in aging and a decrease in revenue. You may also notice that you have problems with a specific insurance payer, having higher aging amounts for that payer. You could have an issue in your eligibility and benefits process, a credentialing error, or patient intake issues among many other possibilities. Knowing how to read your aging report can point you in the right direction to identify and resolve systematic errors in your billing process.

Denials are common contributors to high aging report values. Using the detailed view of your aging report, dates of service that have been denied should be recorded in a designated document for follow-up. You will want to record as much information as is necessary about the patient and date of service, as well as information from the EOB or ERA regarding the denial reason. You should also have a place to log all follow-up activity until the claim is resolved, paid and posted, or deemed unresolvable.

Patient Aging Report

Similar to your Insurance Aging Report, the Patient Aging Report will show any patient balances that are unpaid, filtering out amounts that are owed by insurance. The patient aging report will include balances owed for any private pay patient that you see, as well as patient responsibility for sessions covered by insurance.

The information is organized in the same way as the Insurance Aging Report, listing each patient with an outstanding balance and then showing the amount due in columns based on how old the balance is.

As long as you are keeping up with payment posting, the patient aging report can be used similarly to the insurance aging report, as a tool to help you understand which patients you need to follow up with to settle any balances, or as an indicator of procedural problems. If you have large amounts of patient aging overall, you may need to evaluate your financial policy and charge capture process. Is it clear? Does it include what patients need to pay when they come in for a visit or is it ambiguous? Also, do your clinicians or front office staff understand your process and are they equipped to implement the financial policy? If they have any questions or confusion you may need to retrain them on the process and have them start collecting money. Cleaning up your patient aging can help to increase your revenue and profitability, which we cover in more detail in Chapter 11.

CHAPTER SUMMARY

In this chapter you have learned about the importance of accurate record keeping as it relates to payment posting. Achieving payment from your patients or insurance is a huge victory in the life of your practice and is the tangible vote of confidence that you are providing real clinical value to your patients. While it is fun to see the fruit of your labor, ensuring that you are maintaining your payment posting process is critical for the continued success of your private practice. As a start to thinking about this process, here is what we recommend doing to solidify your strategy:

Follow-Up Actions to Take:

- When you receive an EOB/ERA, read it thoroughly and make sure you understand what you are reading
- Set aside time to payment post if you haven't outsourced this process
- Deposit paper checks promptly if you receive them
- Create a standard document to record denials and future follow-up activity
- Create a written process that you follow when payment posting

Chapter 10:
RCM STAGE 6: CLAIM FOLLOW-UP

C **laim follow-up** is the process of identifying claims that have been submitted and have not yet yielded any remittance, and investigating the status at the insurance company. It can also refer to resolving claim denials and rejections. Claim follow-up helps ensure that you are accurately reimbursed for the services you provide to your patients. Proper claim follow-up can also help identify any issues or discrepancies in your billing and coding, allowing you to correct them in a timely manner.

The process for following up on claims, like many processes within insurance billing, requires time and attention to detail. You will first need to be able to identify which claims require follow-up, decide the best course of action based on the claim status, and manage and record follow-up activity until any issues are resolved and closed. In this chapter, we will cover all of this information as well as the importance of claim follow-up.

IDENTIFY WHICH CLAIMS REQUIRE FOLLOW-UP

We learned in Chapter 9 that EOBs and ERAs will provide information on denials. This is a very straightforward indicator that a claim will require follow-up and includes information on the patient, the date(s) of service, and the denial reason. You will also need to follow-up on any claims with EOBs or ERAs that you believe were processed incorrectly. Another direct indicator of the need for follow-up is if you receive rejection notices in your EHR.

By referencing your insurance aging report summary and detail reports, you can identify additional open claims that need follow-up that may have slipped through the cracks when processing EOBs or ERAs. This should capture any denials and rejections, as well as claims that have not yet had payments posted, claims that you believe were processed incorrectly according to a patient's benefits or your fee schedule, and sessions with progress notes that have not been completed and therefore no claim has been generated.

A good rule of thumb is that any claims less than 45 days old should not yet require follow-up, unless you have received a rejection notice or EOB or ERA that indicates otherwise. This is because it can take up to 30 days from claim submission for a claim to process through the insurance company's system. If you find that you have a payer that regularly processes claims within 2 weeks, then you may want to customize your follow-up date range accordingly, but 45 days old is a good starting point.

We recommend that you start with your oldest, largest aging amount to follow up on first from the insurance aging report summary. This is because the older the aging, the less likely it can be for you to actually receive payment. Using the insurance aging report detail, you can view a list of sessions that make up that oldest largest amount of aging. There is likely a report that shows the Insurance Aging Report detail within your EHR. If it doesn't I would highly recommend reconsidering your EHR as this is an invaluable feature. For each claim that is open you will either need to post a payment, investigate information on the EOB or ERA you believe to be incorrect, generate a progress note for a claim to be submitted, resolve the rejection, or resolve the denial.

Compile a List of Claims that Need Follow-Up

Using the indicators above, you can compile a list of all claims that require follow up. You will want to include as much information about the session as possible, including things such as date of service, patient name, patient insurance and ID number, the rendering provider (and likely their NPI and Tax ID), any information you have from a denial or rejection notice or discrepancies on an EOB or ERA, and the date that you discovered an issue.

As you continue follow-up, this document will be constantly updated with progress and next steps. You will also add new line items as new issues are discovered, and remove line items as issues are resolved.

DECIDE THE BEST COURSE OF ACTION FOR EACH OPEN DATE OF SERVICE

For each date of service that requires follow-up, you will need to identify what the next step is to close the claim.

Post a Payment

For claims that have been processed but not yet closed, determine whether you have an EOB or ERA that needs to be posted. If so, and you determine the EOB and ERA information is correct, you can post the payment and close the claim. This is why we stress the importance of payment posting before any follow-up activity is completed. It will save you time in the follow-up process. Ideally you are encountering very little payment posting in Claim Follow-Up. If this is not the case, you may have an error in your payment posting process.

Investigate EOB/ERA Discrepancies

If you determine that you disagree with information that was on the EOB or ERA such as the allowed amount or the patient responsibility, make detailed notes on your follow-up document including details of what you disagree with. Call the insurance company to investigate. You will want to record reference numbers and any important information provided by the insurance representative, and record your next follow-up action until the issue is resolved and payment can be posted correctly.

Complete Progress Notes

For sessions that do not yet have a progress note, you will need to evaluate your timely filing limits. For sessions that are still within timely filing, develop a plan for yourself or the clinician responsible for creating the progress notes to ensure that these are generated. You will want to work from oldest to newest so that claims can be submitted as soon as possible. For claims that are outside of timely filing limits, there is not much to be done. This becomes lost revenue for your practice.

Resolve the Rejection or Denial

Rejections and Denials are the more complicated forms of follow-up. They are an inevitable part of insurance billing, but by establishing good processes throughout all stages of revenue cycle management, you should be able to minimize the number of denied and rejected claims. In the following sections, we will cover how to approach denial and rejection resolution in more detail.

HOW TO RESOLVE A REJECTION

A claim rejection occurs when there's a demographic error or an insurance error that the third party clearinghouse identifies and notifies you of before the claim gets to the insurance company. You will want to understand the reason for the rejection, obtain any missing information and correct and resubmit the claim until it is accepted.

Understand the Rejection Reason

Typically there's a notification within your electronic health record system that alerts you to the rejection. You will want to look for a rejection code in your EHR that will tell you why the claim was rejected. If there is no rejection code or reason, you can call the payer and ask.

A key difference in rejections versus denials is that you would talk with the payer's EDI department rather than the claims department, because rejections mean the claim hasn't entered the adjudication system so the claims department won't have it.

Common reasons for a claim rejection are the date of birth for the patient is wrong, the insurance is invalid (possibly due to an incorrect ID number), a claim was submitted with a duplicate date of service, or even that the name of the patient is incorrect. The smallest error can cause a claim rejection and therefore cause problems with the claim process.

Correct and Resubmit the Rejected Claim

Once you have the reason for rejection you need to make the correction. You may be able to find the issue and fix it internally without having to check with your patient or with the insurance company. You'll want to refer back to the relevant information and documents the patient provided in the pre-registration or registration phase. Verify the information against the information that was submitted on the claim. Typos happen, whether it be during the claim creation process, or when patient data is entered into your EHR system. Sometimes you may need to get updated information from your patient or you may need to verify the provider information submitted on the claim against what you were credentialed with.

Once you've identified the error you can fix the claim within your electronic health record system and resubmit the claim. The important part here will be making sure that the claim actually goes through the system and does not reject again. If the claim is rejected a second (or even third) time you'll have to follow up once more.

HOW TO RESOLVE A DENIAL

The claim rejection process is meant as a way to prevent claim denials, but every demographic error is not always caught, and there are some reasons for denials that a clearinghouse will not be able to catch since they are more procedural within the insurance company. For denials, you first need to understand the denial reason, correct and submit a corrected claim if you can easily do so or work with a representative who can reprocess the claim with the correct information, and in the event of continuing denials you may want to appeal the denial.

Understand the Denial Reason

If your EOB or ERA indicates that the claim has been denied, the first step is to understand why it was denied. Carefully review the denial notice you received from the insurance company to determine the reason for the denial. If the information that was provided is unclear, you may want to contact the insurance company to get an explanation that you can understand so that you can take action to fix it. Instead of the EDI department like for a rejection, you would want to contact the payer's claims department for information on denials.

Denial reasons vary widely. They include but are not limited to issues with the diagnosis, treatment plan, or patient demographic information provided, insurance issues, missing modifiers, incorrect provider credentials, a lapse in insurance coverage, or a duplicate claim submission. Some denials are easier to fix than others.

Submit a Corrected Claim for the Denied Claim

Errors on claims may be obvious, such as an incorrect modifier or an incorrect patient ID number. In these cases, you correct the errors and send in a **corrected claim**, also referred to as an **amended claim**. The corrected claim indicates that it is replacing the previously denied claim, preventing the corrected claim from being rejected as a duplicate. This is when having a current image of the patient's insurance ID card can come in handy- you can use it to reference patient information on the claim in comparison to their ID card. In some instances you may need to reach out to your patient directly for updated information to send in a corrected claim.

You will want to document every step that you take to resolve a denial, and assign due dates to follow-up activity until the claim processes and payment has been received. At this point the practice should finalize the claim by posting the payment and ensuring the client has been charged if necessary. This may involve updating the patient's records and reconciling the account to ensure that all charges have been properly credited.

Continuing Denials

You may discover that some denials are unresolvable. If the claim has been denied rightfully and the client owes the full amount, you should explain the reason for the denial to your patient. You can also provide them with information on how to appeal the decision if they think it is incorrect.

If you have done everything you can to fix the claim and it is repeatedly denied or you do not agree with the denial reason, you may choose to appeal the denial. This may involve submitting additional documentation or requesting a reconsideration of the decision. It is important to keep track of all communication with the insurance provider and to document any additional steps taken to appeal the claim. At the end of this process, if the claim appeal does not result in payment, the patient will owe the outstanding balance. You will want to inform the patient of this possibility early on so they do not incur a higher balance.

THE IMPORTANCE OF CLAIM FOLLOW-UP

Claim follow-up is not only a way for your practice to ensure that you are collecting all revenue that you are owed, it is also a way for you to identify errors within your revenue cycle management. As you are following up on claims, look for patterns in errors.

If you have several claims that have EOB and ERA information that does not match what was learned on an E&B check across multiple insurance companies, you may have a problem in your Eligibility and Benefit check process.

If you are receiving a high number of denials related to provider information for one insurance company, you may have a credentialing error.

If you have one provider who is consistently not completing notes, you may need to adjust that provider's schedule or provide additional training.

These are just a few examples of issues that we have been able to help providers discover through a forensic claim follow-up process. Once an error has been identified in your billing system, you can take steps to resolve the problem and avoid future claim rejections, denials, discrepancies in information, and timely filing risks.

CHAPTER SUMMARY

In this chapter you have learned about the reality of claim follow-up. Claim issues are going to happen in your private practice career. You are going to find that working with insurance can quickly become overwhelming and stressful if you do not have a consistent process for following up and resolving claims issues. This part of the billing process is the most time consuming and may be one of the biggest reasons you might outsource your billing to another company. Here are some tools to help you set up the process to make claim follow-up better:

Follow-Up Actions to Take

- Create time in your calendar for claim follow up

- If you outsource your billing, create time in your calendar to review the claim follow-up work your biller is doing
- Promptly obtain information from your patients to resolve rejections or denials
- Maintain a clear record of your follow-up activities
- Communicate clearly with your patients about any claim issues that may impact their part of the session

Chapter 11:
RCM STAGE 7: OUTSTANDING PATIENT COLLECTIONS

The final stage of Revenue Cycle Management is following up on any unpaid patient balances. In spite of the best efforts and processes, these balances can accumulate for several reasons. This includes an eligibility and benefit check not being completed prior to a session, or a claim processing differently to what an eligibility and benefit check indicated, such as a patient only paying a copay when they actually had not yet met their deductible and owed the full allowed amount for the session.

Collecting money from patients can be an uncomfortable aspect of running a mental health practice. It is important to establish clear payment policies and communicate them effectively to patients in order to avoid misunderstandings and conflicts. In this chapter, we will discuss various options for collecting payment from patients, including setting up payment plans, and accepting different forms of payment. We will also address common challenges that may arise when collecting money from patients and provide strategies for handling them. Whether you are a solo practitioner or part of a larger practice, the information in this chapter will help you effectively and fairly collect payment from your patients.

WHAT TO COLLECT

The EOB or ERA received from the insurance company should indicate what a patient owes according to their benefit plan. You can verify this information against the E&B check information, keeping in mind that E&B checks can sometimes be incorrect. If you have any reason to doubt the information on the EOB or ERA, you can contact the insurance company to learn more. Typically, the amount shown on the EOB or ERA should be collected from the patient.

You can reference your patient aging report detail to see whether or not payment was collected from a patient for a session, and if it matches what is indicated on the EOB or ERA. If a session still shows an open patient balance, you will want to collect what is indicated on the EOB or ERA from your patient.

If you have patients that agreed to private pay sessions, you will want to charge them your established cash rate for the session. If you have established a sliding scale agreement, you would charge your patient according to the sliding scale that you have established.

HOW TO COLLECT

In the event that you don't collect from your patients during the charge capture phase and you notice that the balances are starting to pile up, you can utilize a few strategies that will get you paid for the work that you have done.

Catch Up With a Patient the Next Time They are In-Office

The next time that your patient is in your office, check their balances and make sure they are caught up. Be prepared to explain any outstanding balances based on eligibility and benefit checks, ERA or EOB information or your patient's insurance plan. This may lead to some uncomfortable conversations with your patients but it is critical that they catch up paying your practice. You can't work for free and the patient understands that reality.

You may need to set up a customized payment plan with your patient to cover any balances.

Once the patient leaves the office, your chances of collecting any outstanding bill drop significantly. Therefore, it is critical that you have a process for receiving funds before the patient leaves the office.

Set Clear Expectations

You should have a clear and effective policy regarding outstanding patient payments that you communicate to your patients as part of their patient intake. If your patient is aware of the process regarding outstanding balances in advance, then they will not be surprised if you need to follow up with them later.

Remember that people forget! Sometimes people start to drift from the original expectation that you set for payment. Make sure that it is clear to the patient that the expectation for payment is going to be upheld per your informed consent paperwork and that you will continue to repeat the expectation so they don't forget.

Keep in mind that if people have a clear expectation of what is expected from them financially it is very possible that you can maintain a clean patient aging report in your practice. This helps to avoid needing to employ a collections agency and allows you greater freedom in your practice to focus on your skills.

Always Keep a Card on File

It is a good idea to keep a card on file even if the patient is going to pay via another method of payment. The reason this is important is because it allows for you to maintain some control over the cash flow of your practice. If you don't have a card on file, you don't have any recourse in charging the patient for missed or late sessions. Keeping a card on file allows you to maintain financial autonomy in your practice.

Additionally, keeping a card on file allows your patient to forget that they have to pay. This can be an element that provides peace of mind for them as they seek to use your services. By taking away the payment step for your patient they can focus on what they came to see you for and you never miss a payment.

Keeping a card on file, for most people, is a win-win scenario!

Sending Statements

There are many different ways that you can send statements and payment reminders to your patients, including digital reminders and mailing paper statements.

Digital reminders such as email or text message have the benefit of being able to include a link for a patient to submit payment electronically. Making payment easy makes it more likely for a patient to do so. Digital payment reminders are a cost effective way to get your patient's attention regarding unpaid balances.

If you need to send paper statements, start with normal colored paper. If you don't get a response, change the color of the paper that you are sending to your patients such as red paper to indicate urgency. You can also buy a stamp that says "Outstanding Balance" or "Final Notice" so you can stamp the envelopes before you send them.

People throw away mail that doesn't look imposing and your statements might be going to the trash. Do something to get their attention and allow them to focus on the outstanding balance that you have.

Make sure that any statements you send have clear instructions on payment methods. It can be helpful to offer multiple ways for a patient to pay you, either by mailing a check, calling in with credit card information, or accessing a payment portal online.

Hire Someone to Collect Patient Balances for You

If collecting from your patients is difficult for you, you can fastrack payment from patients to your practice by hiring someone to collect those balances. Practice Solutions offers a service where you can send out statements to your patients and patients can call in to pay their balances. This allows you to avoid some of those uncomfortable conversations and allows a trusted third party to do the collecting for you.

Finally, if you have patients that you are no longer seeing who have outstanding balances, you could hire a collections agency that allows greater leverage in collecting payment although using a collections agency should be a final step on the road to collecting money from your patients.

CHAPTER SUMMARY

In this chapter you have learned about what patient aging is, what to collect, and how to collect the amounts that your patients owe you. Understandably, this can be one of the most uncomfortable parts of your practice. Keep in mind that your patients are seeing value in your services and want to pay you for the good work you are doing together. To help cut through some of the ambiguity of collecting from patients here is what we recommend:

Follow-Up Actions to Take

- Talk about what your patients owe to make sure they are aware of their responsibility
- Always collect a credit or debit card
- Charge cards after each and every session
- Send statements to the patients that haven't paid you
- Hire a collections agency if you are unable to collect from problem patients

Chapter 12:
FINAL THOUGHTS

Insurance billing is important for private practice owners to understand, but involves a lot of time and effort to manage properly. Practice Solutions offers several options for providers who are looking to advance their practice and achieve their business goals.

FURTHER READING: ADVANCED BILLING TOPICS

This book provides a basic understanding of insurance billing and the revenue cycle management process, but there are more advanced topics that you can learn as you develop your billing processes. Practice Solutions posts weekly content on our blog that can provide you with additional resources and educational topics related to insurance billing, such as

- Coordination of Benefits
- Primary and Secondary Billing
- Working with Medicare and Medicaid
- Ongoing Practice Management
- Balance Billing
- Adjustments in Insurance Billing
- Billing as a Supervisor or Under Supervision

If you found this book helpful and are interested in further developing your insurance billing knowledge, be sure to subscribe to receive emails when new blog content is published and for announcements regarding future educational resources at www.practicesol.com/blog.

PRACTICE HEALTH CHECK

You can use the topics covered in this book to develop processes for your practice. If you would like the eyes of a professional to check your processes, evaluate the financial health of your practice, and gauge your success in revenue cycle management, Practice Solutions offers Practice Health Checks. To learn more, you can visit

INSURANCE BILLING SERVICES

Any provider who reads this book in its entirety is miles ahead of the rest in terms of understanding insurance billing, but that does not necessarily mean that you have the time to manage it on your own. Practice Solutions can remove the burden of billing from you and your practice, allowing you to focus on patient care. Your education in billing will make it that much easier to have a productive working relationship with one of our billing specialists. To learn more, visit www.practicesol.com.

GLOSSARY

Adjusted Amount: The difference between the submitted rate and the allowed amount.

Allowed Amount: The allowed amount is the amount that the insurance company is indicating is allowed as payment for this service. This should match the contracted rate on your fee schedule.

American Medical Association: An organization founded in 1847 with the mission "to promote the art and science of medicine and the betterment of public health." The AMA developed the standardized system of CPT codes that are used in medical billing.

Blue Cross Blue Shield: An insurance company unique in that it is operated independently in each of the states that it operates in.

CAQH: A database for provider information. CAQH profiles are designed to provide standardization among providers, and to aid in the credentialing process. Your information on CAQH must be verified or updated quarterly. Simply review the demographic information that is on file and make sure that it is accurate, or make any necessary changes. CAQH is also another great resource for information on the insurance industry.

Clean Claim: A claim that processes on its initial submission.

Centers for Medicare and Medicaid Services: Part of the Department of Health and Human Service, it is the government organization responsible for regulating Medicare and Medicaid health plans. Whether or not you are a Medicare or Medicaid provider, we strongly recommend checking in with cms.gov to stay informed about insurance legislation, processes and trends.

Clearinghouse: A third party entity that verifies all information submitted on a claim before it arrives at the insurance company. If any submitted information does not match what the insurance company has on file for you as a provider or your patient, the claim will be rejected and sent back to you for correction.

Contract: Upon completing credentialing, you should be sent a contract outlining the terms of your professional relationship with the insurance company, including responsibilities about timely filing of claim submission, reimbursement rates for services, and contract renewal advice. Keep this document handy and securely stored.

Contracted Rate: The rate that the insurance company agrees to pay healthcare providers for any service provided to a member of their plan.

Coordination of Benefits: A form that a patient submits to each insurance company if they have multiple insurance plans to designate which insurance is primary, and which insurance is secondary. For claim submission, it is important to follow the chain of submission as outlined in the patient's coordination of benefits.

Corrected Claim: A claim submitted to replace a previously denied claim, also known as an amended claim.

CMS-1500: A standard paper form established by the National Uniform Claim Committee to submit insurance claim information from a provider to an insurance company. The form is a specific shade of red. You can purchase claim forms from a variety of sources including office supply stores or direct from a government printing office.

CPT Code: A code used to designate a specific medical treatment or procedure for billing purposes. The American Medical Association developed, published, and updates CPT codes.

Credentialing: The process of applying to be an In-Network provider with an insurance company.

Date of Birth: Used on insurance claim forms to identify plan members, you should always keep your patient's date of birth on file, as well as the date of birth of the insurance policy holder if your patient is covered under a parent, spouse, or other guardian's plan.

Deductible: An amount designated by a patient's insurance plan that a patient must pay for healthcare services before some benefits of their plan will apply. Copays do not typically apply toward a deductible.

Denial: A claim submitted to the insurance company is denied when the services rendered are not covered under the patient's insurance plan. Claims can be wrongfully denied, in which case appeals can be submitted for further review. Check out our article Standard Denial Reasons and How to Solve Them if you are experiencing issues with claim denials.

Electronic Data Interchange: The electronic version of a CMS-1500 form. Electronic Data Interchange connection must be securely established between your EHR, a clearing house and the insurance company in order for claims to be submitted electronically. Electronic Data Interchange is HIPAA compliant.

Electronic Funds Transfer (EFT): A direct deposit payment into your bank account from the insurance company.

Electronic Health Record (EHR): This term can refer to individual records of electronic health data, but more often refers to a software system that contains all of your patient data.

Electronic Remittance Advice: The electronic version of an explanation of benefits. ERA information is transmitted securely to your EHR system for posting against a claim. The ERA will include all of the information that is typically included in an explanation of benefits.

Eligibility & Benefits Check: Sometimes referred to as Verification of Benefits, the act of checking a patient's insurance plan to see if and which medical services are covered under their insurance plan, and the patient payment responsibility for any given service. Can also be helpful in determining whether or not a patient has met a deductible or out of pocket maximum.

Employer Identification Number (EIN): A number assigned to business entities by the IRS, similar to a social security number for tax reporting. Your Employer Identification Number must be included on claims if you credentialed yourself or your business using your EIN.

Explanation of Benefits: Once a claim has been processed at an insurance company, an explanation of benefits will be returned to you and/or your patient outlining what the insurance company paid, or what a patient is responsible for paying. If a claim has been denied, further information will be included on the Explanation of Benefits.

Fee Schedule: A document, usually listed in a table, of CPT codes and their corresponding rate that an insurance company has agreed to pay a healthcare provider for services rendered. The fee schedule is proprietary information to the insurance company, and is not to be shared among providers. For further reading, check out our blog post What is a Fee Schedule?

Good Faith Estimates: Estimates of costs of services provided to your patient that are made with the best of your knowledge.

Health Insurance Portability and Accountability Act (HIPAA): Legislation enacted in 1996 to protect patient health information. With the development of electronic data sharing, HIPAA was designed to make sure that patients could have peace of mind knowing that their data is secure. For therapists, there are many available HIPAA compliant technologies that you can use in your practice so that you do not have to think twice about being HIPAA compliant.

If You've Credentialed With Insurance It's Time to Comply With HIPAA. Here's What That Means.

Health Maintenance Organization: A type of insurance plan which requires patients to first see their primary care provider before they visit any specialist, and patients must see an in-network provider to receive coverage.

HIPAA Consent Form: A form that the patient fills out acknowledging that their PHI can be shared with an insurance company in order for insurance claims to be processed.

In-Network: A healthcare provider is considered In-Network when they are credentialed with the insurance company in question. Typically, patients will seek a healthcare provider who is In-Network with their insurance plan since the patient can take advantage of better benefits.

Insurance Aging Report: a report of insurance sessions that have not yet had payments posted and are considered "open."

Insurance Card: A card that belongs to the patient with information about their insurance plan.

Medversant: A database for provider information. Your profile is designed to provide standardization among providers, health plans, and government organizations to aid in the credentialing process. Most insurance companies that accept CAQH information also accept Medversant profiles.

National Plan & Provider Enumeration System: NPPES assigns NPI numbers to providers upon registration. You must have an NPI number if you are submitting claims to insurance. This is another online database that has provider information on record. NPI information is stored here for each provider, and the information can be publicly accessed. Your information should also be reviewed regularly on the NPPES website to make sure that all information is accurate.

National Provider Identifier: Your NPI number is one of several important identifiers for you as a therapist. NPI numbers are assigned by NPPES. You can apply for either an individual NPI number, also referred to as a Type 1 NPI, or an NPI for an organization or group, also referred to as a Type 2 NPI number. You may also have both. It is important to know which NPI number was used when you credential with an insurance company so that claims can be submitted using the same NPI number to process properly.

No Surprises Act: Legislation that took effect in January of 2022, the No Surprises Act was established to prevent patients from receiving large "surprise" medical bills. Providers are required to provide a Good Faith Estimate to their patients before services are rendered.

National Uniform Claim Committee: Developed and regulates the CMS-1500 form for claim submissions.

Out-of-Network: A provider is considered Out-of-Network if they are not credentialed with the particular insurance company in question.

Out of Pocket: What a patient will pay for healthcare services themselves before their health insurance plan will fully cover medical expenses. An Out of Pocket Maximum is the maximum amount that a patient will pay in a given year, including their deductible and any copays or coinsurance amounts, before their insurance company will cover 100% of medical expenses.

Payment Posting: Recording the payment information from the EOB or ERA or any external patient payments into your EHR for corresponding sessions.

Prior Authorization: Some services require authorization from an insurance company before the insurance company will provide coverage on those services for their patients. A request must be submitted to the insurance company including diagnosis and treatment plan.

Protected Health Information: Under the HIPAA Act, health records for patients are considered private information that must be transmitted securely to any healthcare organization with the patient's consent. This includes demographic information, diagnosis and treatment plans for your patients.

Preferred Provider Organization: A type of insurance plan which allows a patient to see a specialist without referral, and allows coverage of services provided by Out-of-Network healthcare providers.

Rejection: A rejection of a claim occurs at the clearinghouse, before a claim arrives at the insurance company. A rejection is usually due to a demographic error, including things such as an incorrect NPI, Tax ID, address for the provider or the patient, or an incorrect date of birth. Rejections can be corrected and resubmitted.

Revenue Cycle Management: The term used to describe the stages of insurance claim submission, from the moment that a patient decides they would like to see you for services, to claim submission, follow-up, collection and payment posting. Revenue Cycle Management is what Practice Solutions specializes in. Our team is specialized in handling the stages of Revenue Cycle Management so that healthcare providers can spend the most time with their patients.

Social Security Number: A number assigned to you by the IRS for tax reporting purposes. You may use your Social Security Number as a tax ID when you credential with an insurance company if you are credentialing as an individual rather than as a business.

Standard Rate/Cash Rate/Private Pay Rate: The rate that you establish for your services to patients who are paying privately and not using insurance. Standard rates are up to you to decide. Standard Rates are different from your contracted rates established by the insurance company.

Tax ID: An identifier for your business assigned by the IRS for tax purposes. Tax IDs are used by the insurance company to identify you as a provider in the processing of claims.

United Healthcare: According to ValuePenguin, UnitedHealth Group controls the highest percentage of market share in the insurance industry. One of the key players in the world of insurance.

www.ingramcontent.com/pod-product-compliance
Lightning Source LLC
Chambersburg PA
CBHW070624030426
42337CB00020B/3910